Beat the Odds

Winning ideas for smart gamblers

Tim Phillips

brilliantideas

CAREFUL NOW

The title of this book suggests that if you're smart you can beat the odds. But no matter how smart you are you still have the risk that you will lose money: that is why it is called gambling. We can't guarantee you will make your fortune, so take care, and use that intelligence of yours. Don't gamble money you don't have. Don't gamble when you don't have the time. Don't commit money if you don't have any idea how likely you are to see it again. If you even suspect that your gambling is not under complete control, stop immediately and get advice from the organisations we list inside.

We list a lot of websites; they might change from time to time. If they do we apologise – but much of the information you will be looking for is available on the web from many different sources. Also we stared at the calculations and rechecked them until our heads hurt – but if we have made a mistake with our probabilities let us know and we will correct our sums as soon as we can.

Copyright © The Infinite Ideas Company Limited, 2008

The right of Tim Phillips to be identified as the author of this book has been asserted in accordance with the Copyright, Designs and Patents Act 1988.

First published in 2008 by
The Infinite Ideas Company Limited
36 St Giles
Oxford, OX1 3LD
United Kingdom
www.infideas.com

A CIP catalogue record for this book is available from the British Library.

ISBN 978-1-904902-66-9

Brand and product names are trademarks or registered trademarks of their respective owners.

Designed by Baseline Arts Ltd, Oxford
Typeset by Sparks, Oxford – www.sparkspublishing.com
Printed in India

Brilliant ideas

Brilliant features

Each chapter of this book is designed to provide you with an inspirational idea that you can read quickly and put into practice straight away.

Throughout you'll find three features that will help you get right to the heart of the idea:

- *Here's an idea for you ...* Take it on board and give it a go – right here, right now. Get an idea of how well you're doing so far.

- *Defining idea ...* Words of wisdom from masters and mistresses of the art, plus some interesting hangers-on.

- *How did it go?* If at first you do succeed, try to hide your amazement. If, on the other hand, you don't, then this is where you'll find a Q and A that highlights common problems and how to solve them.

Introduction

Any adult with money to spend can gamble. Not many of us gamble intelligently, but your principles might save you from wasting your money. Here are the five rules that help me and will help you too.

THE FIVE PRINCIPLES OF SMART GAMBLING

I'm not going to promise to make you rich. But I will promise that if you follow the tips in this book when you gamble, you will be better off than if you ignore them. I can't guarantee that you will be dealt the cards you need, or that your horse won't fall at the last fence, or your team's goalkeeper won't unexpectedly drop the ball – but when you do hit the jackpot, you'll probably make a better return because of what's in here.

I don't take the credit. The people who patiently gave me advice deserve that. They are people who either live entirely off the money they win, or who just win much more often than you and me. But the more I talked to them, the more I realised that they were giving me the same advice in different forms, using different terms and different jargon, talking about different games – but using the same principles. I've turned this advice into five rules. Why five? Well, ten would have been hard to remember and three would have meant missing out some important stuff.

So, you know you're a smart gambler if:

You do your research. You wouldn't buy a pair of jeans without trying them on, looking in a couple of shops and having some idea what you were looking for. If you couldn't find the right jeans, you'd go home and try somewhere else. On the other hand, most of us bet good money when we simply don't understand what we are getting. There's plenty of statistical analysis that, if you know what you're looking for, can save you money. Use it, because if you work at your gambling, you'll be better off. It's up to you how much work you do.

You understand the game. Smart gamblers know the percentages and the odds of winning when they bet. They know how big an edge the house has, they know the rules and if there's an optimum strategy, they know what that strategy is. They can spot when they're outmatched and they know when they're on top.

> **Lisa: 'I'm a monster!'**
> **Homer: 'No, Lisa, you're not a monster. The only monster here is the gambling monster that has enslaved your mother, and I call him Gamblor! We must save your mother from his neon claws!'**
> *THE SIMPSONS*

Defining idea…

You play the right stakes. Always manage your bankroll. You don't always bet thinking you will win; you gamble when you think the return you will get is better than the risk you will take. Smart gamblers sometimes bet high and sometimes bet low, and don't bet at all if there's no obvious value.

You get the best value. Gambling is a competitive market, so get the best reward for the risk you take. Different bookmakers offer different prices. Different casinos pay out using different values, or have different house edges, or use different rules on different tables. There are loyalty schemes and incentives that will return some of their profit to you. Different poker betting strategies will squeeze out different returns from other players. Unless you compare the odds and act to take advantage of them at the right time, you're literally giving money away. If you want to get the best value, compare the form with the bookmakers you have accounts with or simply go to www.oddschecker.com. You can't ever guarantee that the odds won't change, or that you checked everything, but given a choice between 5–1 and 6–1, I know which I'd choose.

You are always in control. Emotion is your enemy. When you watch poker tournaments on TV, the players are often rigged up to heart-rate monitors. When the players make a big bet, the heart rate shoots up – but they rarely make a rash bet, no matter how much adrenaline is flooding their system. Angry gamblers, desperate gamblers, excitable gamblers and distracted gamblers are bad gamblers. It can be tempting to imagine that gambling is simply mindless speculation, but for the experts, nothing is further from the truth. Smart gambling is founded on knowing when to go all in and when to pick up your chips and walk away. If you can't control yourself when you gamble, the most profitable advice I can give is to close this book now and go and find something cheaper to do with your spare time.

Each one of these principles can improve your bankroll. When you're gambling, try to concentrate on applying one or more of them until they are second nature. For many professional gamblers, a 'gut feeling' isn't an emotional response – it's their unconscious mind quickly sizing up the situation and sending a warning if they're doing the wrong thing, or reassuring them that they're getting every last drop of value from their bet.

What could be simpler? Well, quite a lot. Gambling is hard work – as hard as you like to make it. It can also be a bit of fun. What you get out is, in a large part, dependent on how much you want to put in to these five areas.

1

What's your goal?

It's better to be a smart gambler with £50 and a clear idea of what you want to do than £50,000 and no strategy.

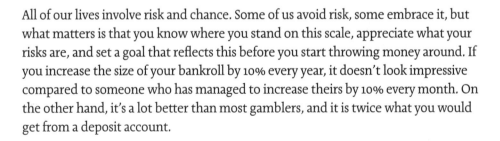

Intelligent gambling isn't about where you start, it's where you finish. And it's not about getting rich — it's about matching your performance to your expectations.

All of our lives involve risk and chance. Some of us avoid risk, some embrace it, but what matters is that you know where you stand on this scale, appreciate what your risks are, and set a goal that reflects this before you start throwing money around. If you increase the size of your bankroll by 10% every year, it doesn't look impressive compared to someone who has managed to increase theirs by 10% every month. On the other hand, it's a lot better than most gamblers, and it is twice what you would get from a deposit account.

So there's no absolute standard. The first and most intelligent decision you can make is to set yourself a goal that you can achieve. If that goal is too low, it won't be interesting; if it's too high, it will just encourage you to be reckless and act out of character.

Here's an idea for you...

All serious gamblers keep a log of what they did, why they did it, and what the outcome was. It has two functions. The first is as a reference for you, to stop you doing the bad things twice and to help you spot the good things. The second is as a route map towards your goal: plotting daily or weekly winnings and losses, examining the success of one tactic compared with another, means you have an honest assessment of how well you are doing against your target.

We're seduced by the idea that gambling is easy money. It isn't. We read the stories of poker players who pull in huge jackpots, punters who earn a fortune at the racecourse on one afternoon or neighbours who snag all the money they will ever need on the lottery, and it looks like a wonderful shortcut to the good life. Just wanting to be them is not a realistic goal.

On the other hand, gambling isn't much fun if you accept that it will cost you money. It's worth setting a target that means you have more money at the end than the beginning – otherwise it's a lot less effort to put your cash in the bank.

Where do you pitch your goal? It has to recognise your level of knowledge. If you are new to racing or card rooms or casinos, then you might get lucky on your first outing, but you probably won't on your second, third or fourth. If you earn a return of 10% on the cash you employ when you are betting, you're doing as well as many professionals; but that means to earn £100 in a day, you need to bet £1000 and be prepared to lose it. Setting an arbitrary goal that you must come home with £100, and betting frantically to try and reach that goal, is asking for trouble.

You also have to respect the potential for winning that the game offers. Roulette, as we will find out, is not a beatable game. You can't play it for money. Blackjack is –

just, but it requires skill and commitment. Poker offers consistent winning opportunities but a lot of competition. If your retirement plan is to win the lottery, you're a sucker. Add up the margins, look at the capital you have available, look honestly at how well you've been doing up to now and do your sums.

You need to budget your time. You have a job, a family, some friends and some hobbies. Respect them. Gambling can take hours out of a day – if you neglect your other commitments it's bad for them and worse for you. That's the start of a gambling problem.

Finally, you need to be honest about how you are going to get to your target. Some of the methods – spread betting or no-limit poker, for example – are high-risk and high-reward. Others – premium bonds springs to mind – offer little or no risk and a lower reward. If you want to double your money in six months, premium bonds are unlikely to do it for you. But if you're going to do it by spread betting, it's possible. You just need to be extraordinarily talented.

So set your goal: you want to make a specific profit in a certain time. You're going to give a definite number of hours a week to it. You're going to mix some low risks and some high risks, or try to learn a new skill. Write them down, stick with it, don't get discouraged if you lose at first.

And here's one final goal: enjoy it. The minute hard work turns to tedium, adrenaline turns to stress and gambling starts to control you rather than you controlling it – that's the time to cash in your chips.

'I suggested we flip a coin, but Angela said she doesn't like to gamble. Of course by saying that, she was gambling that I wouldn't smack her.'
JENNA FISCHER playing Pam Beesly,
The Office USA

Defining idea...

3

How did it go?

Q **I don't know anything about gambling. What's my target?**

A   *To find out whether you like it and what you like. Put aside a small bankroll as the cost of your education to buy the books you need and to try playing small stakes. Be open to everything and, after a couple of months, you will have a clear idea of what you like and whether you have the talent. This isn't for everyone. Then you can start thinking about profit.*

Q **My life is boring. If I gamble at night, I can live a little. Is that a good goal?**

A   *It's a dangerous one. When you gamble, whether you're naturally conservative or not, you need to be yourself. If you can't easily contemplate risk in your day-to-day life, you are unlikely to be able to evaluate it and act intelligently when you gamble. If you're bored there are many steps you can take, but acquiring a double life with a gambling habit shouldn't be one of them.*

2

Don't trust luck

If you're gambling regularly, there's no such thing as luck. There's only statistics and chance: the rest is down to you.

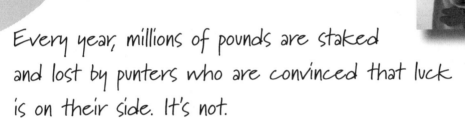

Every year, millions of pounds are staked and lost by punters who are convinced that luck is on their side. It's not.

To gamble successfully, you have to understand the way that statistics can help you, that unpredictable stuff can undermine you, and that there isn't a some intangible force looking out for you.

We've all had days when we've been lucky. An event we've been dreading is cancelled at the last minute, our irritating relatives decide not to come and stay after all and you bag the last ticket for the football. Most of us would agree that this didn't happen because you put your left sock on first, because Mercury is aligned with Jupiter, or – as tradition decrees – because you had a haircut when there was a new moon.

If you believe that your fortune as a gambler is guided by these events, then you've got no business reading this. You should have spent the money on a rabbit's foot instead. Cross your fingers, bet only on a Monday or a Thursday, don't leave a bel-

Here's an idea for you...

If you're really convinced that something is 'lucky', then try an experiment to prove it. Compare what you would win over a period of time using your 'omen', compared to a random pick or the efforts of your cat. Be honest and note down the losses as well as the wins and you will be surprised how quickly your 'luck' runs out.

lows on your kitchen table, hope that your shoelace keeps coming untied, never give a present of scissors – do all of these, but please don't make bets based on these random events and expect a good return on your stake.

Short-term 'luck' is a fundamental part of betting. When the little roulette ball picks your number, it is such a random occurrence that it is impossible to explain your good fortune any other way. But sit at a roulette table for a month, and your 'luck' will dissipate as the laws of probability assert themselves. If you feel some affinity to a number and you prefer to play it at roulette, then go ahead. Just don't

attribute a one-off fortunate event to an outside force that you think, because you have done something to please it, is looking after your financial well-being.

It's easy to confuse luck with something less exotic: for example, you pick a horse in the office sweepstake for a big race because you think blue is a lucky colour for you and the jockey is wearing blue. The horse wins. Good for you, but this possibly has more to do with the fact that blue is the colour of the fabulously wealthy Godolphin stable, which has a strike rate of about 20% and over the years has consistently won the biggest prizes in the sport. So it might be luck, but Sheikh Mohammed bin Rashid Al Maktoum, who spends more on his horses than any other owner, would disagree.

If someone is winning consistently, you could attribute it to 'luck' and sulk because you're not equally blessed. A sensible punter would look for a pattern in what the other person is doing. Often, we assume someone is 'lucky' when there's actually something we can learn from them. It's like the famous quote from Gary Player: 'the harder I work, the luckier I get'.

If you're still convinced that you're just unlucky, ten years of research from Professor Richard Wiseman at the University of Hertfordshire should give you comfort. He has interviewed and researched thousands of 'lucky' and 'unlucky' people, and found that 'their thoughts and behaviour are responsible for much of their good and bad fortune'. He isolated the habits of consistently 'lucky' people and performed an experiment where a

'Luck never gives; it only lends.'

Swedish proverb

Defining idea...

control group was instructed to behave in this way for a month. At the end of the month, 80% were happier and felt 'luckier'.

Professor Wiseman's tips for being more 'lucky' aren't difficult to follow. He suggests we should be open to new experiences. For a gambler, trying something fresh to refine and improve that 'edge' is a fundamental part of a winning strategy. Second, every day, take some time to remember things that went well. Consciously isolating good bets and wins can help you figure out the difference between what's working and not working. Thirdly, visualise yourself being lucky before an event that you have control over, such as a poker tournament. This will help you play with control and confidence, and make you less likely to indulge in desperate bets or over-react to a bad beat. It can't alter the cards you will get, but it might make you just a bit stronger as a player.

Finally, he advises us to listen to our gut instincts; for a gambler, that's potentially dangerous if you don't apply the other principles above and do your analysis: what he means is, listen to your own thoughts and don't get obsessed with outside forces you can't control or over-react to setbacks.

Ultimately, you can't control chance. Things that are outside your knowledge or control will always play a part in whether you win or lose. Put all your effort into the things you can control, think positively and creatively, and you're more likely to come out on top compared to someone who invests importance in lucky charms and celestial omens.

Q   **When I visit a casino, there's a screen that shows the last numbers that came up on each table. Sometimes a colour or a number keeps coming up. Should I bet on that number?**

How did it go?

A   *Because of its construction, a roulette wheel is almost impossible to bias towards red or black, or a number, or even numbers. Probability sometimes throws up what seem like patterns; that's more an insight about how our brains try to make sense of disconnected occurrences than a guide to what will happen next. In short, ignore the screen.*

Q   **My mates are always luckier than me at race meetings. What's going on?**

A   *A few things: first, people love to crow about their wins, and gloss over their losses. Someone who wins on several races might be backing more than one horse and hiding their losses. Second, it's easier to win on several races if you back at short odds – but just as hard to make a profit on the day. Third, you might have a friend with a method that he's not telling you about. Stop worrying about other people and find your own edge. Make your friends jealous of you instead!*

9

3

What's your bankroll?

Never gamble with money that you don't have, or risk money that you need for food and the mortgage.

Gambling uses money, or at least something with a financial value. But as you will see, if you're gambling with your watch, your car or your house, you're not gambling intelligently.

There's a phrase for bad bankroll management: it's called throwing good money after bad. So the first decision to make when you gamble is how much you're going to gamble with. Just as you go into a shop with an idea of what you're prepared to pay for your new shoes, you need to know how much cash you're prepared to play with when you gamble. This is what we call your bankroll, and its size will help to determine how you play.

There are two measures: how much you have to give to gambling overall, and how much you'll commit at any time. Be mindful of both. If you have £2000 for the year, sticking it all on number 23 on a roulette wheel on 1 January is probably not going

Here's an idea for you...

Set up a bank account specifically for your bankroll that you top up every month by standing order. When you know how much there is in that stash, you can work out intelligently how much to commit to each race or event while leaving yourself something in the kitty if the worst happens. It's tough at first to make these judgments, because you convince yourself that every bet is a sure thing.

to give you much fun for that year. But if you do that and lose, don't go back to a casino until you have fresh money to spare.

Be realistic, not everyone can be a high roller: if you start with £20 and leave with £40, that's only £20 gain – but it's a 100% profit. Don't waste time wishing that you had committed £10,000 that you didn't have, and certainly don't bet that £10,000. Bad bankroll strategies include borrowing money from friends, maxing out your credit cards or selling a kidney.

Many regular gamblers are surprisingly conservative. One I spoke to, who never goes near a casino with less than £1000, always likes to have forty times the value of his blackjack bet in his starting bankroll.

Good bankroll decisions are made early and stuck to, because if you rethink, you'll only renegotiate your investment upwards. If you win early, you'll be tempted to think you're 'on a roll', and invoke some supernatural power to convince yourself that you should be playing for big stakes. But you're no better at gambling than you were that afternoon. If a god exists, it's a pretty good wager that he or she doesn't care whether you win at cards.

If you lose early, racecourses and casinos have plenty of ATMs so you can lose some more by trying to win your cash back. Betting shops are not far from banks, and online betting sites will allow you to deposit more cash. Resist the temptation to replenish your bankroll as hard as you can. Be patient.

So how do you calculate your bankroll? Never, ever, play with money that's needed for something or someone else. The phone company or your mortgage lender isn't going to be sympathetic. You have responsibilities to provide for people close to you and to be honest with them. You need self-respect to provide for yourself too. If you have no disposable income, don't gamble until you do.

If you can spare some cash, work out how much. Give yourself an allowance and, if you have a partner, tell them what that allowance is. Always be honest about how much you are betting with the people it affects.

Don't think your budget is just about cash. How much time will you spend in casinos, at racecourses, in betting shops, on the Internet or studying form? How much will you spend on tips, statistics, tickets, computers and trips? All of this comes from your bankroll too.

A long time ago, my mum had a professional gambler for a boyfriend. She had a great time with him, because when he won, they'd celebrate extravagantly and they would go to posh restaurants and shops. That was how he liked to live. When he lost, they would go to cheap restaurants, and laugh about his bad luck. But here's the thing: he always had enough left to go to some type of restaurant with her. That's bankroll management.

Defining idea...

> **Roy: 'If you need money, how come you play poker?'**
> **Oscar: ''Cause I need money.'**
> **Roy: 'But you always lose.'**
> **Oscar: 'That's why I need the money.'**
> **Roy: 'Then don't play poker.'**
> *THE APARTMENT*

How did
it go?

Q I like to bet on heavy favourites. Surely to get a good return I need to commit all my bankroll?

A *The temptation to go 'all in' all the time can be overwhelming, but resist it. I once bet my entire bankroll, heavily odds-on, on Michael Portillo to become leader of the Conservative Party. I'd spent weeks carefully building those profits, and when I lost I had nothing but empty pockets to show for it.*

Q I won £10 at the races, but it cost me £20 to get in. Am I a winner or a loser?

A *It's up to you. If you had a good day, then maybe it's an expense, just like going to the pub. If you're going racing every weekend, that's pretty expensive. What matters is that you're honest about the state of your finances.*

4

Sometimes you lose

Your strategy was perfect and you still lost. Clever punters understand that the most important thing is to learn a lesson and incorporate it into their strategy – and move on.

Face it, you can't control everything. Sooner or later, you'll have a losing night. The question isn't so much 'Will I lose?', it's 'How will I cope with losing?'

The answer you give to that question will go a long way to making you the smart gambler you want to become.

Just before the 2003 Rugby World Cup, I had an in-depth chat with Sir Clive Woodward – or as he was then, plain Clive Woodward. For those of you who have been living under a rock for a few years, England, under Sir Clive, went on to win the World Cup. At the time I spoke to him, Sir Clive had won thirty-one out of thirty-five matches and was coaching the favourites for the tournament. But he spent a lot of his time talking about losing; about how when you take chances, they don't always work out.

Here's an idea for you...

One of the 'Sir-Cliveisms' that his players lived by was 'T-cup' – thinking correctly under pressure. Sometimes we're under pressure: we've lost a lot of money and we're not getting the cards, or we're tempted to put everything on the seventh race to make up for what we lost on the first six. This is the time to remember your mantra: repeat to yourself 'T-cup, T-cup' and do what you know is the right thing to do in that situation. Don't be ruled by the frustration you feel at losing.

'The moment you think you are not learning, you will come second,' he said to me. 'You have got to be pushing forward for new ideas.'

Next time you have a bad run of losses, think about this, from Sir Clive: 'Coping with failure is easy. As long as you can look in the mirror and know you are doing everything possible, coping with loss is not difficult.'

How do you know you're doing everything? By being analytical, win or lose. 'I look at why we are winning games. If you have won a game, that is the time to look closely, analyse it, what you did, how you prepared – especially the big games. If you lose a game, you don't over-react. Look at it, but don't over-react … and yet it occurs to me that most of us do the opposite.'

Sir Clive wasn't giving me advice on how to be a better gambler, but if I'd have listened a bit more closely, he might have saved me a bit of cash in the last few years. The trick is, win or lose, to analyse what happened afterwards in exactly the same way: don't congratulate yourself or beat yourself up, but ask the right questions. When you bet on a horse to win and it *just* gets beaten at the post, you can kick the cat – actually, don't do that – and bemoan your bad luck, or you can try and work out why that happened and act on your insight. You've just paid to learn a lesson about this horse: maybe it doesn't prevail in a tight finish. That means maybe back it each way next time out or, if the next race contains a few plucky fighters, steer clear of it completely.

The alternative is to say, 'I nearly had a winner there, I was unlucky, let's back it again.' You might have a point: the horse might have been hampered, or the jockey didn't push on enough. But if you don't look, you'll never find out.

Sir Clive again: 'If we succeed it is because we did a hundred things 1% better. The attention to detail is an easy step to make. It is simply getting those one per cents. Why does one [team] win and one come last? It is what I call the critical non-essentials, the one per cents, hundreds of those that make the difference. I am a sponge. Anything that will give you an extra 1% – that's what it is all about.'

In our world, there is simply no rule for where the 'one per cents' can be found – because if there was, everyone would do the same thing and they wouldn't be advantages any more. But one reliable way you can learn from your mistakes is to recognise your weaknesses and train yourself to take a breath before repeating them – break the cycle in which you lose, blame luck, and then do the same thing again. For example, if you find yourself trying to fill a straight at poker when the odds are against you – you have 5, 6, 8 and 9 and are wishing for a 7 – it is not bad luck that beats you, it's the statistical improbability of getting that card. Next time the opportunity presents itself, stop yourself from acting on impulse.

'The pressure will be on, but as long as we think correctly, we can handle it and still enjoy it.'

SIR CLIVE WOODWARD

Defining idea...

When we lose, we prefer to think that it 'wasn't our day' or make excuses. You won't always find the answer if you try to analyse why you lost your bet, but it can show you that the influence of conditions, tactics or location might be more important than you thought. This sounds like hard work. It is. But these extra one per cents are the hard work that wins World Cups and are also the difference between loss and profit for you – so it's worth taking notice of.

How did it go?

Q   Isn't it better to hate losing?

A   *Given the choice, losing isn't as good as winning. But that's the point: when it happens, you don't have the choice. You don't have to like it, but that money's gone, no matter how much you wish you had it back.*

Q   How do you cope with losing?

A   *This from a semi-pro gambler: 'When I bust out in the casino, I go to the pub, forget it and buy the first round for everyone. If you complain all the time when you lose you'll have no money and no friends either.'*

5

Quality, not quantity

There's no need to bet on everything that moves. Whether it's horse racing or poker, blackjack or football, good gamblers know when to say 'no'.

It's a rule that applies in industry, too. You can compare the most influential business leaders to gamblers who know what they're doing.

A couple of years ago I met one of the people who is effectively revolutionising business in the UK. Martin Bolland is one of the partners at private equity firm Alchemy Partners and his job is to look at risks – and decide when to take them. So he's a good man to ask about taking on a bet.

Private equity deals in big risks. The firms buy companies that have fallen on hard times, change them, and sell them again. It's a controversial business, because those changes often mean big job cuts or chopping up the business into small parts and selling each bit, but the UK's private equity firms have been making a lot

Here's an idea for you...

The search for quality is even more important at the poker table, where a sure sign of mediocre players is the habit of investing small sums in poor hands – based on the slim hope that if the right cards come on the flop, it's a winner. Most often, middling cards come. Your hand is OK, but there are plenty of hands that would beat it. Really poor players go on calling other people's bets on the basis that they've got to chase their original investment. There's a rule of thumb that some players follow: never call someone else's raise unless you would have been prepared to raise first.

of deals. The way it's presented in the press: they are snapping up anything that's on offer, like a compulsive gambler trying to find a greyhound to back in every dog race. Talk to Bolland though, and he's working on the opposite assumption.

His overwhelming advice is to invest less often in higher quality investments.

For all of us who have seen an advertisement for a great tipster promising fabulous winnings if only you call his premium rate phone line, remember Bolland's tip: 'Suspend your natural inclination to purchase from a good presenter. The toughest deals to assess are the deals that come with a slick presenter, who is highly articulate … Make sure you are not equating a good presentation with the belief that it must be a good plan … I'm almost happier when a company is presented badly to me.'

Some professional punters bet every day, but some of the most successful place a dozen huge bets a year. The way you prefer to gamble is down to your personality, but really outstanding value is extremely rare.

Years ago, my family knew a guy in the local pub. He didn't have nice clothes, a job, a good house or much of anything. But he could pick a horse.

Every few weeks he had a tip, always on a horse that was 20–1 or more. Not many people took him seriously at first, but you couldn't help but notice how often his tips came in. On the other hand, you couldn't ask him 'Got any horses today?' because, as he pointed out, there wasn't value like that around every day.

How did he do it? It helped that he spent every hour of the day reading the form guides pinned on the wall of the bookmaker's shop and watching the races, and so understood more about racing and horses than you or I ever will. He also had a lot of time on his hands, and not a lot of money to invest, so he eked it out by taking few chances.

I can credit him with my biggest ever win. By the time the message had been passed on to me the horse had already come in from 100–1 to 33–1, but the money our family and friends put on even at that price paid for several holidays. Maybe today he's big in private equity.

'You got to know when to hold 'em, know when to fold 'em, Know when to walk away and know when to run.'
KENNY ROGERS

Defining idea...

21

He understood that quality is rare, but the relentless search for a quality risk is the mark of a ruthless gambler.

This can tax even the toughest gambler. In poker you can be 'dry' for an hour or more as your stack of chips slowly dwindles. But playing mediocre cards rather than folding them is an expensive way to beat boredom. It is tempting to talk yourself into making a bet when there's no value to be had, but you have to retain your objectivity. Indeed, the illusion that you can somehow 'control' an external event, rather than just control the amount of money you gamble on it, is a symptom of problem gambling.

As Bolland says: 'The ability to walk away is key. Part of the ability to make a good deal is the ability to say "It's time we knocked this on the head and moved on" … Anyone prepared to fudge these assessments probably cannot measure their own success.'

Q   How often should I bet?

*A   There's a trade-off. For example, if you're placing twenty bets a day, you
don't have time to do analysis on the value of most of them. If you're
betting once every three months, you might have done a lot of work, but
you're not getting much action and a couple of unlucky results will cripple
your bankroll. The rule of thumb is in between: don't bet unless you can
explain exactly why you're investing.*

Q   Which tipsters should I use?

*A   Look in the papers and you can believe that four horses have a good
chance in every race. Premium rate phone tipsters, TV analysts and even
the sports reporters on Radio 4's Today programme all recommend horses
to bet on. If you like a tipster, follow their advice – but only when you do
your own analysis and reach the same conclusion and only when the price
is right.*

How did
it go?

23

6

The urge to splurge

Gambling can be addictive. Learn to look out for the danger signs and how to pull yourself back from the brink before it's too late.

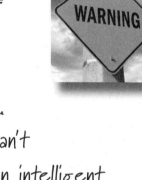

As savvy gamblers know, intelligent gambling sometimes means not gambling. It's all about control — if you find you can't exercise that control, then you're not an intelligent gambler.

Worse than that, you might have a problem. If that's the case, the smartest thing you can do is take an honest look at yourself and, if you need it, get help before you hurt yourself and the others around you. Does this sound dramatic? Yes, but it's a serious problem for some people. There are 175 Gamblers Anonymous groups in the British Isles, and the Gambling Commission produced a report in 2007 that showed there are about 250,000 problem gamblers in the UK.

Here's an idea for you...

Perhaps the biggest indicator of how you feel about gambling is how you feel when you are *not* gambling. For the problem gambler, the intervals between gambling binges can often feel irritating and frustrating. They feel nervous and insecure, longing for the security of being a 'player' again. Get into the habit of analysing your emotions honestly and not making excuses, and if you're slipping into bad habits, take a complete break for a few weeks to rediscover the real world.

The good news is that this figure hadn't increased from the last survey, eight years previously. The bad news is that if you're one of the 250,000, that doesn't really matter. And many others would say this is a huge under-estimate, as online gambling makes it possible to hide a problem for longer.

How can you tell if you have a problem? There are several questions you can ask yourself. Is your gambling affecting your work or your home life? Are you 'stealing time' from other things so that you can gamble? Many problem gamblers keep their problem a secret by inventing excuses and stories to explain where they were when they were simply in the betting shop, at the casino or even up all night playing online.

Win or lose, the problem gambler has a strong desire to return quickly. If you lose, you feel a pull to go back and recover your losses. If you win, you feel the same pull to go back and win even more. Both desires are irrational – what happened before has no bearing on what will happen the next time you gamble. But it's also an attribute of the problem gambler that he or she creates a 'dream world' in which they have control over their environment. They can 'will' a win in ways that they can't control the outside world.

How are you handling your bankroll? Good bankroll management is the most important attribute of an intelligent gambler. Bad bankroll management is never smart, but if you are selling things to provide money for gambling, borrowing cash that you can't pay back from friends and relatives to gamble, or – worst of all – stealing to provide funds for gambling, then you have a problem and you need to get help.

What do you do with your winnings when you win? Many of us fantasise from time to time what we would do if we had a big win. We would buy a car, go on a holiday or maybe surprise our families (who might be most surprised that we've actually walked out of a casino with more money than when we went in for once). This isn't a symptom of a gambling problem as much as a symptom of a fertile imagination, but it can lead to problems. If, when you win, you are reluctant to use your winnings for anything except gambling; if a win is never enough, and you insist on chasing more profit every time; if you enjoy the feeling of being the 'big shot' that you're unable to hang on to your winnings, then this is problem gambling – not least because that big fantasy win will never happen. You'll hang on to your winnings for a day and then gamble them all away.

If you have a problem, then you need to do something about it now. Stop reading this, for one thing – it's not for you, and might never be for you. Ask for help from professionals who will help you diagnose your problem and start you on the path to recovery. But be warned: taking a test on a website and feeling remorseful is rarely enough. You may need counselling.

'Every form of addiction is bad, no matter whether the narcotic be alcohol or morphine or idealism.'
CARL JUNG, founder of analytical psychology

Defining idea...

You might find that if you are worried about your self-control, you have an ally in the industry. Casinos and betting shops don't want problem gamblers as customers because problem gamblers often end up causing problems for them as well. Casinos, for example, will let you 'self-bar' yourself, and refuse you entry – or restrict your access to chips. If, however, you have got to this stage, you probably need more help than the gambling industry alone can offer you.

How did it go?

Q   I might have a problem. Where do I go for help?

A   *Fortunately there are plenty of options available. Gamblers Anonymous is listed in the phone book. You can get help and information from GamCare's website (www.gamcare.org.uk), or on its confidential helpline (0845 6000 133). Your doctor can help – as can your family and friends, if you let them. Online casinos and bookmakers will have a link to information and help.*

Q   I know I gamble too much, but how often should I gamble?

A   *There's no rule. Gamblers Anonymous members take an absolute line: even buying a lottery ticket or tossing a coin is too much. Counsellors can help you find your level.*

7

What do the odds mean?

When you compare the prices on offer, they're not always presented in the same format. Learn how to quickly translate from one format to another and you can spot the best price.

While it's in the bookie's interest to encourage us to bet by making things simple, they don't always make things as simple as they could.

One of the classic problems for the occasional punter, and one of those nasty chores that you have to learn to be able to know what you are betting on, is to understand what odds mean so you can get the largest return. You thought that the mental arithmetic that your grandparents leaned at school was a waste of time, didn't you? I can't claim this Brilliant Idea is going to be the most exciting you will ever read, but you have an incentive to get to grips with it.

Essentially, betting is taking a financial risk. The size of the risk is expressed as the odds. If you don't know how to calculate the odds, you don't understand the risk you're taking, and no one thinks that's intelligent gambling.

If you're going to a racecourse, comparing online odds between exchanges and the betting shop, or just sitting in front of the afternoon's racing on the TV, make yourself a little ready reckoner. (Sometimes bookmakers give pre-printed ones away, but writing out your own will help you learn the odds.) List the odds in ascending value and their decimal equivalent. Keep it in your wallet. Your mates might find it amusing at first, but they'll be grabbing it out of your hand after a few pints.

First, the traditional odds that you see on British horse races are the multiple of your stake that you will win – but remember, you get your stake back too. So: 2–1 (or '2–1 against') means you will profit by double your stake, plus your stake. £20 turns into £60. At 3–1, it becomes £80. 'Evens' is 1–1, which doubles your money – the odds equivalent of the toss of a coin.

Not all odds are so neat. 12–5 means that for every £5 staked, you will make £12 profit – that is, get £17 back. So £20 turns into £68. But is this higher or lower than 5–2? Quick! Before the price changes! And is 7–2 higher than 10–3? When it's seconds before the off and you need to get on, it's hard to compare prices to get best value.

There's no easy way to do this, other than by becoming familiar with the way odds move and trying to think of them as top-heavy fractions. Often a horse will move in a progression, for example if there's a lot of money going on it. So a horse's odds could start at 3–1 (the equivalent of 12–4 or 24–8) becomes 11–4 (22–8), then 5–2 (20–8), then 2–1 (16–8) and then 15–8. Smart gamblers don't do sums like this – they know by instinct how this works, the same as knowing whether a flush beats a straight at the poker table.

Then there are odd-on bets, which express the probability (as opposed to possibility) that the horse, dog, team or individual will win. Think of it as the fraction upside down. For example, '3–1 on' means you get your stake back plus one third extra: if your stake is £20, you'll get a return of £26.67.

Relief comes in the form of decimal odds, which are often used overseas and increasingly on the Internet. Decimal odds are really the only useful way to express the minute fluctuations in price on a betting exchange, but they are not, repeat not, just the decimal representation of traditional odds. The number you see is how much more money you will have if you win – a dividend. So evens is not 1.0, it's 2.0. (Don't take a bet at 1.0. It's literally a no-win.) 11–4 is 3.75. You can change fractional odds to decimals by dividing the fraction and adding 1.0, so 5–2 is 5 ÷ 2 + 1, or 3.5.

This can make your head hurt, especially in close handicaps or when you've had a couple of drinks. It's like trying to work out the best mobile phone tariff on stage at the Albert Hall with your old maths teacher shouting 'Come on!' in your ear. This is one more reason why having an intelligent betting strategy that you have thought out in advance really helps. Instead of trying to keep up with every price, you simply follow a few that you are interested in. For example, if you think a boxer is only good value at 3–1 and he is currently at 5–2, you don't have to worry about betting on him when he moves to 11–4 – except as a hint that the price is moving your way. However, it would be useful to watch for the price hitting 4.0 on the exchanges.

'Chance favours the prepared mind.'

LOUIS PASTEUR

Defining idea…

How did it go?

Q   How do you work out a 'double'?

A   *If you make a double bet (two bets linked together), remember that you can't get your return by multiplying the odds. Imagine that one is at 2–1 and one is at 4–1. The double is 8–1, right? Wrong. It's the return on the 20–1 bet placed at 4–1. For a £100 stake, that's £300 multiplied by five, or £1500. That's why decimal odds are so much easier, because those can be multiplied together (3.0 × 5.0 = 15.0).*

Q   When I went to a high street bookmaker, the horse was 10–1, but when it won I was paid £80 back for my £10 bet!

A   *Prices move all the time. If you think that the price will reduce before the race starts, ask to take the current price when you place your bet. In this case, the horse was 7–1 at the start of the race and not taking the current price cost you £30 – but if it had started at 12–1, you would have made £20 more again. Any bets without a price marked on them get this 'starting price'.*

8

Online poker

Some of the world's top players earn a good living at their laptops. It's exciting, potentially profitable and a lot more interesting than playing _FreeCell_.

If you want to play poker online, and all serious poker players do, then you're not exactly stuck for choice.

You don't have to hang around looking for action – indeed, on some of the more popular sites, you might have to queue for the table of your choice at busy times.

The bad news is that there are millions of online poker players competing against you. The good news is that most of them at the low-stakes tables aren't intelligent gamblers, and so while you will sometimes win and sometimes lose, a disciplined online poker player will not find it an expensive hobby – and it may prove to be a profitable one.

If you're looking for online poker rooms, then first you might want to try the poker room of your online bookie. Otherwise, stick to the big sites: Party Poker, Full Tilt,

Here's an idea for you...

Online poker rooms usually offer a no-stakes table. It's good for learning how to play, but when you play poker it has to matter when you lose. The trouble with playing no-stakes is that the people there are often literally messing around, throwing in meaningless bets. They're easy to beat, but you won't find players like them very often in the real world. Try a small-stakes pot limit game instead to brush up your tactics – you have to play really badly to lose heavily in a 10¢ or 20¢ game.

Betfair or four or five others – www.casino-choice.co.uk carries reviews of the big sites. When you sign up and enter, you will see a list of the current games in play. This list shows how many people are sitting at each table and their screen names, how many seats are free or how many people are queuing, what the stakes are, and probably some statistical data such as average pot size and number of hands per hour.

When you're starting out, you need to be careful about your choice. If you decide to join a high-stakes game, for example with a $5 or $10 no limit, then $50 isn't going to go far. You'll end up out of the game before you had a decent hand to play. Also, if you opt for a game with a high average pot size, you've got a chance to win big – but also to lose big.

You'll probably be up against some aggressive raisers, and unless you're confident you have their measure, you don't want to mix it until you have some idea of what you're up against.

If you're learning the ropes, don't sit at a table where there are 120 hands an hour being played. When you're an expert, by all means play four high-stakes games at once in different windows on your PC. Right now, all that will happen is that you will lose four times as fast.

Also, it's a good idea to set yourself a time limit as well as a bankroll. When you're wrapped up in online poker, hours can drift by – especially if you are playing well. Take your time – don't try to win the World Series of Poker in one night.

Online games take some of the calculation out of betting, allowing you to raise the pot or go all in at the click of a button. Here's a problem: most players click that button far more often than if they had to physically move a pile of chips. Do this and you are what poker players call a 'fish', adding money to pots you can't win. When you finally get cards you can win with, you'll not have enough chips left to make them count.

Another thing to bear in mind is that online poker doesn't sit you in front of a real-life player, and so it's easy to get wrapped up in your own cards. You stop thinking about how your opponents are playing, or even what cards they should be holding. 'I'm not very lucky tonight,' a player messaged me recently when other players were happily taking his money online. 'I keep getting good hands, but everyone gets better ones.' In reality, his mistake was committing too many chips without considering why we were calling his bets.

At the beginning, online poker can seem like a blur of cards and chips. But it's not just a potential money-earner – it's a great learning tool, as long as you play to your best strategy and remember that you are playing against real people with strengths and weaknesses.

Defining idea…

Harry: 'Thought you were going soon.'
Carter: 'Soon. When you've lost your money. Won't take long.'
Harry: 'Clever sod, aren't you?'
Carter: 'Only comparatively.'
GET CARTER

35

How did it go?

Q   How do the online sites make money from me?

A   *They take a fixed percentage of each pot, called the 'rake', or an entry fee to a tournament. It soon adds up, even though you don't notice it.*

Q   Which site is best?

A   *If you want to improve, any busy site attracts serious players, even at low stakes. They also have blogs, tips, loyalty schemes and regular big tournaments. Try a few to see which interface you prefer.*

Q   How do I know the standard of the other players online?

A   *In general, the best players play for higher stakes. Some sites such as Full Tilt highlight the games where their professionals are playing and you can watch them and marvel at the thousands of dollars that are zipping back and forth. Occasionally you will walk into a great player at low stakes. Losing your chips is the price of your education at their hands.*

9

A free lunch

Bookies splash around bonuses and incentives so that we'll stick with them. Sometimes they can turn a good bet into a sure thing.

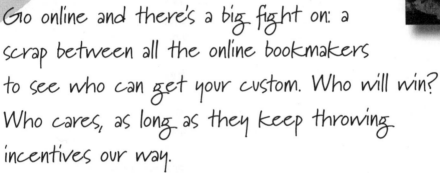

Go online and there's a big fight on: a scrap between all the online bookmakers to see who can get your custom. Who will win? Who cares, as long as they keep throwing incentives our way.

Internet economics puts great store by the acquisition of customers – even more so for the online bookmakers, who are desperate for you to sign up with them. The reason is simple: if odds are more or less similar across the board – as they often are these days – then the lazy punter is likely to visit the usual website that they gamble on and put the money on there. And because the bookies make most of their money from exactly that type of punter, it pays for them to attract as many as possible.

Here's an idea for you...

When you pick up these bets you get the chance to do a little arbitrage of your own – a no-lose bet. Say, for example, Sunderland are playing Manchester United in the Cup Final and one bookmaker offers 4–1 against Sunderland winning. It's generous, because they realise that many occasional punters can be tempted by big odds on the big game. A rival is offering only 3–1 against Sunderland but 4–1 on for Manchester United to win and a £20 free bet if you sign up. You use the free bet on Manchester United at 4–1 on to cover your losses: if you lose, you lost nothing except a free bet. If you win, you are £25 up. So that means you effectively have a free bet of £25 on Sunderland at 4–1 against. If Manchester United win, you break even; Sunderland win, your profit is £100.

That's why, when you go to websites dedicated to sports, gambling advice or – most of all – to comparing the bookmaker's odds, you will find lots of advertisements for online bookmakers promising you free bets to come and play with them. Some of the freebies are quite boggling: £25, £50 or £100 of free bets are possible, particularly on major horse races such as the Grand National or the Derby. It's really like getting a cheap room in Vegas – if you stay at the hotel, you're going to gamble there.

Online casinos will also offer you incentives to go and play. This is a reason to go and play with them but it's not a reason to play more than you otherwise would have done. Remember, most games in an online casino are an empirical demonstration that the house always wins – but you don't have to feel so bad if they're just wining back their own money.

We're at an advantage because we are not suckers. We use our discretion and only go to the place with the best odds, because we are intelligent gamblers. We wouldn't sign up for one of these incentives, would we?

Of course we would. A £25 free bet is a £25 free bet. We're playing with someone else's money. Even if you have to commit your own cash as well, it still changes the odds dramatically. For example, betting with £20 of your own money at evens means you either profit by £20 or lose £20. If you have a £10 free bet and £10 of your own money at evens, you either profit by £30 or lose £10. It's effectively become a 3–1 bet.

There are disadvantages to this. First, you will be required to deposit your own money, so taking too many of these bets splits your bankroll into little bits and makes it harder to manage – especially as some of those bookmakers have higher margins and so worse odds on offer. If you have accounts with 20 bookmakers, it's hard to know whether you're winning or losing. On the other hand, if you like to compare the odds, then you'll be coming back one day soon for another bet. And if you want to use your incentive at an online casino, then the odds on roulette, for example, are the same more or less everywhere.

Also, you might be tempted into making silly bets. Just because the odds have changed, it doesn't always make the bet a good one. In the previous example, a 3–1 bet might still be poor value if your analysis says that the horse is even more unlikely to win. If you blow your incentive bet on some flight of fancy, you're no better off.

On the other hand, they're giving us something here. We'd be fools not to take it.

Defining idea…

'*I'm happy doing what I'm doing, and if you have that kind of attitude then everything else from there on is a bonus.*'
TOMMY LEE, rock star

How did it go?

Q **I used an incentive for an online casino but I can't access my bonus at the moment. Why not?**

A *Many online casino incentives have to be 'earned out' – they are released bit by bit according to how much you play, like a loyalty scheme. Remember, though: it's money you wouldn't have otherwise had, even if you don't have it yet.*

Q **Where do I find the best bonuses?**

A *Look on sites such as www.oddschecker.com, www.easyodds.com or www.betfinder.com, clicking on a 'special offers' link to see what's available. The bonuses on sites such as these are usually listed in a column on the right of the page and often they change to reflect the big race or match of the day. But wait until there's a bet you want to take – you can only take one free bet with each bookie.*

10

Come racing

Betting on the course might not mean you get better odds, but it's a fun way to make money and a smart punter can pick up profitable information.

If some of the advice I have been passing on makes an intelligent punter's life seem slightly less exciting than stamp collecting, then put some fun back in your bets by going racing and see where your money's going.

I'm not recommending this out of love of a beautiful thoroughbred. I hate horses: they give me asthma and one of them sneezed green goo all over my face when I was fourteen ('Aw! He's got a cold!' my girlfriend said, and chose to comfort the horse), which still makes me wake up screaming. But if you're in a packed and noisy grandstand at a racecourse on a summer's evening, watching your nag charging down the straight towards the finish, straining your eyes for the colour of your jockey's cap in the chaos, you'd have to be dead not to find it exciting.

We agree that intelligent gambling's about enjoying yourself. Believe me, this is fun. Racecourses have the reputation for being a bit snooty, but not so these days

Here's an idea for you...

If you want a cheap and cheerful version of horse racing, go to the dogs. Many of our greyhound stadiums are under threat, which is sad because they can be wonderfully atmospheric places. Most have little restaurants with a view of the finish line where you can get a meal and a drink, and people come to your table to take your bets. Entry prices are cheap and anyone can understand what's going on – so they're good for the kids too.

– unless you decide to go to Royal Ascot, the Epsom Derby or Glorious Goodwood, or one of those expensive posh meetings.

Instead, why not start at a smaller course – maybe an evening meeting in the summer or a Bank Holiday special? Entry prices are cheaper and a lot of the courses now cater for people who aren't, well, horsey. Some of the courses have Indian restaurants and bouncy castles for the hoi polloi. Don't try the latter immediately after the former.

It's not particularly smart to show up and just stick a tenner on every race because you like the name of a horse or because it's recommended in the race card. Do an hour of research the night before and pick your horses carefully. Save your big bet for a horse that you think offers great value and plan a few lesser bets; look for the right odds. On the course you will find the bookmakers standing on boxes down by the rails. Always look along the row of boards where they mark their prices; often, one may try to attract business by marking your horse at better odds than the competition. Others offer little incentives such as paying better odds for the each way bet. You'll always get the odds that were on offer at the time you placed your bet, not the starting price, so you can wait for the price you want and then pounce.

Alternatively you can bet on the Tote. The Tote doesn't offer fixed prices – all the money goes into a pot, the government takes a bit off the top and the winners are paid out as a dividend. The Tote screens show approximate 'odds' that estimate the dividend at the time you're betting, but these can change radically by the off, especially on outsiders. The Tote can sometimes offer better value than the rails bookmakers, but you have no control over the return you get, so it's not a reliable investment. On the other hand, they do have Tote windows in the bar for when that walk to the rails is just too far.

Going racing is a test of your bankroll discipline. It's tempting to start betting on two, three or four horses at a time as you chase your losses. Know exactly how much you're taking with you and don't visit the ATM while you're there. If your horse looks jittery or bored and you don't want to bet it, don't just throw the money at another horse you don't know anything about. Stick the cash back in your pocket and save it for another day. And always calculate your profit and loss afterwards to include your

> *'Horse sense is the thing a horse has which keeps it from betting on people.'*
> W.C. FIELDS

Defining idea…

43

entry fee, the cost of your race card and travel to the course, because that money has to come from somewhere.

There are hundreds of race meetings every year. One must be right for you. I just hope a horse doesn't cover you in snot.

How did it go?

Q   What should I wear?

A   Nowadays most courses have few dress regulations, but they'll let you know if they have. Beware that those that do have regulations for certain parts of the course, or on certain days, will enforce them – whether you have a ticket or not.

Q   Do you get better prices on the course or online?

A   You'll get more or less exactly the same from the bookmakers. The prices in betting shops and online are taken from the courses. On the other hand, exchanges such as Betfair might still offer better value than you could get on the course.

Q   Where do I find out about meetings?

A   The British Horseracing Authority has a search facility at www.british-horseracing.com/goracing/racing/fixtures/find_a_meeting.asp, or you can download a printout of the entire racing calendar from the same site.

11

Viva Las Vegas

If you want to mix your gambling with a little mild hedonism, head for the casino capital. You can even bring the kids.

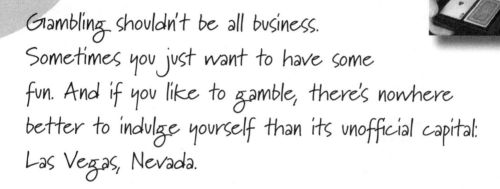

Gambling shouldn't be all business. Sometimes you just want to have some fun. And if you like to gamble, there's nowhere better to indulge yourself than its unofficial capital: Las Vegas, Nevada.

You don't need that much help to gamble in Las Vegas – the entire place is set up to encourage you to indulge. All the big hotels come with casinos attached (there are even slot machines in the arrivals hall at the airport) and you can easily spend your time wandering from one casino to another and totally ignore the other entertainments on offer. I mean, it's not like the Grand Canyon or the Hoover Dam are just around the corner or anything.

The truth is, it's easy to go to Vegas and gamble badly, even for a seasoned punter. The place is set up to give you all the right mental triggers. Despite what you see

Here's an idea for you... **Take out a club card in the casino you visit the most. It's a form of loyalty card: if you play the slots, you put it into the machine before you start. If you are playing a table game, give it to the dealer or croupier when you sit down. Your card will be credited with points, which will eventually translate into small, but pleasurable, freebies (a meal, or a discount on a room). But don't let the card influence how much you play. The discounts are small beer compared to how much you will give the casino – which is, of course, exactly why they offer the cards in the first place.**

on CSI, you're pretty safe from crime on the streets of Las Vegas. Most of the robbery is entirely legal here.

When you book your holiday in Vegas, you might be surprised to find that the hotels, which are usually big, brash and high-quality, are much cheaper than you expect. The food served on giant buffets in the casino hotels is a snip. And if you're gambling, girls in small clothes will bring you complementary drinks at the table for a dollar tip. The owners indulge you: you can gamble all day and all night in nothing more than a thong if you like. It seems too good to be true – and it is, because the house knows that the average punter will pay this generosity back at the tables many times over.

There are tricks to getting out of Vegas without losing your shirt and still having a good time while you do it. Most of them involve some sort of self-control. It's your holiday, but bring your brain. Bring your bankroll too – but decide on a strict budget before you leave. If you want to gamble $1000, go ahead; however, if you lose it all on your first day, don't get another $500 out of the ATMs that are so prominent on the casino floor so that you can win it all back. The problem with being a city where gambling is the number one pastime is that gambling becomes a way of life.

As well as fixing your bankroll, fix your casino schedule. Famously, Las Vegas casinos don't have windows and clocks, so it's easy to lose all sense of time. If you want to pull an all-nighter on the blackjack table, go ahead, but it's better to take a break sometimes. The casinos will still be there when you come back.

Taking time off allows you to clear your head as well. One of the problems of playing for a long time is that you gradually lose your discipline and forget your strategy. If you begin the night by winning, you loosen up and start making side bets that will destroy your stack. If you begin by losing, you sometimes start to throw good money after bad. The casino floor in Vegas is designed to be bizarre: whether it's a recreation of New York, the inside of an Egyptian pyramid, or just a very loud place with lots of flashing lights.

But while most things in Vegas are fake, two things are real. The first is the booze that you are served while you play will eventually cloud your judgment. Some players (especially in the poker room) stick to soft drinks, or at least only have one drink every couple of hours. The other thing that's real is your money. Don't make the mistake that most punters do: play until you lose everything and have to be rescued by your ashamed kids because you fell asleep face down in the buffet. I've seen it happen.

'Las Vegas is sort of like how God would do it if he had money.'

STEVE WYNN, casino owner

Defining idea…

49

How did it go?

Q   Which casinos offer the best returns?

A   *It's a hotly debated topic. Often, to get the best returns on slots, roulette or blackjack, you need to play the higher-stakes tables. Bearing in mind that statistically the house always wins, playing double stakes for a slightly lower 'tax' on your time might not be a sound investment. But sound investments weren't why you went to Vegas. So: if you're playing blackjack, look for tables where they pay 3–2 when you hit blackjack; if roulette is your game, patronise casinos such as the Belaggio and MGM Grand where there's only one '0' on the wheel instead of the Vegas standard two, and the 'En Prison' rule applies. Slots vary dramatically, but overall they are guaranteed money earners for the casino. Those with a statistically small house edge involve you playing big stakes.*

Q   Where should I stay in Vegas?

A   *In Vegas they are constantly pulling down hotels and putting new, increasingly surreal, ones in their place. The main action is on the Strip, where you can stay in hotels that are small-scale recreations of Paris, Venice or New York. You can hop from hotel to hotel as you please. On the other hand, if you want the original, edgier Vegas experience, head for downtown, where the older casinos like the Golden Nugget, Binion's Horseshoe and Fitzgerald's ('The Fitz') are still standing on Fremont Street. They are also where the locals come to play poker and fleece the tourists – that's you – in the poker rooms.*

12

Once in a lifetime

A hot tip, the chance to invest in a business, a mate who knows someone who knows: but is your chance of a lifetime all that it seems? Weigh the odds before you go 'all in'.

I once had a friend who, for some reason, we all called Mike Mango. Mango had an extraordinary stroke of luck: thanks to a local development the value of his flat shot up, and he sold it at the top of the market.

In his mid-twenties he was sitting on £150,000 that he had done little or nothing to earn. At the time, we worked in the next office to a group of friendly ex-traders. One day, one of them came in and talked about a hot tip.

'The shares are about to shoot up,' he said. 'There's speculation about a bid.' Mango checked regularly for the next forty-eight hours as investors speculated and the shares shot up.

Here's an idea for you...

If you want the opportunity of a lifetime, don't be passive in seeking it out. Most of the best opportunities get snapped up by people who've made an effort, gone out to the market and made the right contacts. If you want to invest in business, the British Business Angels Association (www.bbaa.org.uk) can help you or put you in touch with other angel networks. But remember: this is high-stakes gambling and your money will be tied up for months or years.

Two days later, Mango could stand it no longer. Without telling anyone, he pumped the entire £150,000 into this company, just as the investors stopped speculating. Whoever was planning a bid didn't go through with it – maybe they weren't planning it at all – and the shares began to drop like a stone. In twenty-four hours, they lost one third of their value. Mango hung on and hung on before conceding defeat and selling. In one day he lost money it would have taken him two years to earn.

The moral: when someone gives you a 'once in a lifetime' opportunity, it's a gamble; just like putting the money on a horse or the turn of a card. Use our principles of intelligent gambling or you'll surely lose your shirt. Let's see how those principles applied in our example.

■ *Research*: Mango knew little about the company, why someone might want to buy it, and why they might not. It takes time and effort to understand these things. Listening to a bloke in your office isn't research – it's gossip.
■ *Understanding*: Mango knew nothing about the stock market either. He cared mostly that shares were going up, but he didn't really appreciate how fast they could fall too.
■ *The right stakes*: Even our tipster wouldn't have suggested he put his entire bankroll on what, if Mango had asked, he would have conceded was a high-risk punt. When he found out, he was horrified. He didn't feel exactly feel guilty, but in traders any emotional engagement is quite surprising.
■ *Value*: There's a time to gamble and a time when other people have already taken the value. This was that time. Even if the shares had kept climbing and Mango had the expertise to sell at exactly the right time (he didn't), the profit would have been marginal.
■ *Control*: I don't need to explain this one.

Sometimes, especially if you have a reputation as a successful gambler, someone will offer you that chance to invest in their business or will recommend an investment that 'can't lose'. For deals like this, you have access to two experts: an independent financial advisor and your accountant. If you don't know how to read a business

'An investment in knowledge pays the best interest.'
BENJAMIN FRANKLIN

Defining idea…

53

prospectus or a business plan, they do. They can't stop you doing anything, but they can give you impartial advice.

What sort of advice? When you're punting your cash on an idea such as this, you need to know at least three things before you even think about it. First, who's behind the offer? Business ideas need quality people even more than they need quality ideas, in the same way a good horse needs a good trainer and a good jockey. You can judge people by their track record.

Second, you need to know under what terms you are investing: the value and the risk. What do you get and how long are you investing for? Are you getting some extra benefit such as tax relief or a free service?

Third: how much do you know about the market? Eighty British companies go bust every day. The vast majority of restaurants and shops ultimately fail because there's so much competition. Blind optimism and business sense don't often go hand in hand.

That doesn't mean that no investment is good. Unlike Mike Mango, you just need to wait for the right one and be able to accommodate it in your bankroll.

Q   Is it a good idea to invest in your friends and family?

A   It's no better or no worse than any other investment, but it's harder to manage and tougher to extricate yourself from. It's not hard beating your friends for £50 at poker, but it's tougher when their employment, future and houses depend on the result.

Q   I was reading in the paper that ...

A   Stop there. Don't take advice from people you don't know or have no reason to trust other than they seem to have authority. Everyone has an agenda, so always work through it yourself, just as you would the smallest raise in a poker game or a bet on a horse. It's useless blaming other people's bad advice afterwards if you didn't check that advice out.

How did
it go?

13

Getting an edge on the exchanges

On the exchanges you're betting against people like you – so a clever punter knows how to exploit their weaknesses.

Betting on exchanges is a new world if you're accustomed to simple betting. It can be simple, making finding value more straightforward thanks to the way that prices are presented, and complex, because there are many ways to make a profit.

The first thing you need to get an edge on the exchange is a good Internet connection: without doubt you need reliable broadband, because the markets can change extremely quickly. Sometimes there is only £20 or £50 offered at the best price, and if your screen takes thirty seconds to update, you won't get it. Without broadband,

Here's an idea for you...

If you have a guide price you want to get on an exchange, leave it and wait for someone to match it. For example, if you want to bet at 10.0 but the current price is 9.2, leave an unmatched bet at 10.0. But keep an eye open for the unexpected: if the weather changes and the going doesn't suit your horse at all, you'll need to cancel your unmatched bet quickly because it's no longer good value. Many punters forget about these 'orphan' bets and discover to their displeasure that someone – maybe you? – has snapped them up.

you're severely restricting your chance to make a profit.

Many serious punters use software to help them get the best out of the exchanges. This can be complex to set up, but it automates a lot of the tricky processes and helps you track the way the markets are moving. One of the most professional tools is Bet Angel (www. betangel.com), which has a free version with limited functions and a paid-for version with a yearly subscription of £300. It sounds like a lot, but this is a sophisticated piece of software that can help predict how the market will move or make maximum use of your investments. If you manage to use your money more efficiently on the back of a profitable strategy, you can make the £300 back in a few bets. There are many other packages available that are usually less sophisticated but offer some of the same features.

Good software and a reliable Internet connection won't guarantee a profit. You can, however, get a return on Betfair without knowing very much about horse racing or indeed any sport you want to bet on. The fundamental principle of betting on Betfair is to find a price that's out of line with the rest of the market and take it.

The simplest way to do this is to go to a bookmaker's website or visit the comparison pages at www.oddschecker.com, and compare them to what you're getting on Betfair. Do this early in the day, before the market has settled. When you see a Betfair price that's much bigger than the odds you could get at a bookmaker, you can bet on it in the knowledge that the price will shrink. If you like, you can then lay the same horse at the smaller price and lock in a profit.

The second way to get an edge on an exchange is to watch out for over-corrections. Betting 'in running' means betting while the match or race is happening. The odds shoot up and down as punters react to what's going on. Sometimes these can be massive over-corrections – horses can go in and out of the betting in seconds. Intelligent gamblers keep calm and don't over-react, and profit as a result. In a long race, the early leader rarely holds on to the end, and in football, many goals are scored late in the game – but the Betfair odds will overwhelmingly back the status quo. An example is when the game is level, but both sides need the win. Laying the draw and backing either or both of the teams to win will often yield a result. Betfair is a true measure of sentiment: popular favourites (such as Ricky Hatton, the boxer) will often be priced far too low, making whoever they are competing against much better value.

Another way to get an edge is to find obscure markets, lightly traded, where you will find that punters are often not thinking carefully about the form or the specific conditions. If you have some expertise or knowledge – if you're an obscure sports trainspotter – it's easy to turn that to financial advantage.

'You don't learn from smart people, you learn from idiots. Watch what they do, and then don't do it.'
MINNESOTA FATS, pool player

Defining idea…

How did it go?

Q Are exchanges for big-time punters only?

A *Not at all. You can match anything from £2 upwards on Betfair and you can match as much as you like. But remember that you have to deposit the cash in your Betfair account before you bet it.*

Q When's the best time to bet?

A *It doesn't matter as long as you have a plan and work to it. You can bet on a race a month or a day before it – or ten minutes before it or even during it. But there are two times when the market is very volatile: right at the start and during the event.*

14

House edge

Statistically, the house almost always wins. Understanding the house edge and looking for the signs that tell you where the edge is smallest (or non-existent) will give you a better chance to win.

We all think we can beat it, but none of us can. It's the 'house edge' in a casino.

In any game of chance that you will play at a casino, the risks and rewards are calculated so that the casino has a statistically higher chance of making a profit than you do. Or, in plain English: if you play long enough, you just can't win.

Sometimes the house edge is very obvious: the zero (or two zeroes) on a roulette wheel lower the probability that your number will come up. The house edge when you bet on a single number is easy to calculate: in European (single zero) roulette it's 2.7% and in American (double zero) roulette it's 5.3%. The first zero was added to a roulette wheel in 1842 by a two Frenchmen called Francois and Louis Blanc. Blame them all you like, but for 160 years they've had a lot of friends in the casino business.

There are many strategies for beating the house. Most fall into the category of well-meaning misunderstandings of probability theory. You're intelligent. Ignore them. The most famous is the Martingale system at roulette. If you play the Martingale, you bet on one of the areas that gives you an even money payout – black, red, even

Here's an idea for you...

There's one online casino that promises zero house edge. Is this too good to be true? When you play at the Betfair Zero Lounge (go to http:// casino.betfair.com and look for the link), the payouts are graded for a zero house edge. The roulette wheel even has no zero. Why would they do this? Well, it attracts punters who might then play the other games in the casino. Most important, you must play with optimum strategy, all the time. That's not hard in roulette, but it's taxing on the jacks-or-better poker slots or the virtual blackjack table.

numbers, odd numbers, 1–18 or 19–36 – and double your bet each time you lose until you win. So if you bet £1 and lose, the next time you bet £2, and if you lose you bet £4, and so on. When you win, your profit is £1, and then you start again.

There are two flaws with this system. It is mathematically inevitable that at some time you will experience enough consecutive losing bets to bankrupt you, no matter how large your bankroll. In the previous example, if you lost on ten consecutive spins, your next wager is £2^{10}, or £1024, when you have already lost £1023. When you also realise that every roulette table has a maximum stake as well as a minimum – which will also defeat your Martingale – you can see why casinos don't mind Martingale players trying out their method.

The house edge for any table game is tough to work out just by staring at the table of payouts, because it's often hard to work out exactly how often the winning combination will come up – especially when there are special bonus payments and side bets. Many casino enthusiasts provide excellent statistical analysis on their websites. They're a good guide, but take care that the schedule of payouts they're working with is the same as the one that you will see printed on the table in the casino. What looks like a small change – paying four chips for a winning hand instead of five, for example – dramatically alters the house edge for the game, as you will find out when you play. Newer casino card games such as Let It Ride usually have about a 3% edge for the casino, if you play them with optimum strategy.

When you're looking at slots, remember that the house edge is calculated for the game as a whole, and some of the big-paying slots offer a house edge that is theoretically around 1%. That's true. If you were the only player, and you were playing every machine in the network for a long period of time – during which you would have to win the progressive jackpot – you would get back 99% of your investment. Slots are one of the few services that can attract customers by advertising that they will get less back than they put in.

House edge is less important, though, than two things. First, if you bet everything you have, you need to get up and leave. In this case, the house edge is 100%. Second, you need to play the best strategy every time to minimise the edge, and for many games, that takes some learning.

And here we get to the most important thing about house edge: it has only a slight relationship to do with how much money the house makes from you. On a roulette table the edge might be 5%, but the 'hold' – the casino profit – is nearer 30%. Why? Because we tend to keep playing until we lose. Imagine your bankroll as a zig-zagging line on a graph, with ups and downs. The house edge means that the average will slope gently downwards. Unfortunately, as soon as the bottom of one of the troughs on the graph touches zero, you need to go home. That's the way most of us play, and it's not intelligent.

> **'The house doesn't beat the player. It just gives him the opportunity to beat himself.'**
> NICHOLAS 'NICK THE GREEK' DANDALOS, US gambler

Defining idea...

Intelligent gambling can't beat the house edge. But depart from optimum strategy, or play too high stakes for your bankroll and increase the chances that you go bust, and you're literally giving money away.

How did it go?

Q   Are there beatable slot machines?

A   *Jacks-or-better poker slots on some payout tables can be beaten, or the house edge can be shrunk to almost zero. You have to play like an automaton, doing the precise right thing for every hand. Casinos sell little cards of this strategy and some websites publish them – but the strategy, and the edge, changes lightly according to the pay table.*

Q   Are there beatable casino games?

A   *If someone invented blackjack tomorrow, the casinos wouldn't even look at it. That's because the house edge can be shrunk to almost zero, and with skill the house can be beaten.*

Q   I've seen this guaranteed way to win posted on the Internet ...

A   *Stop right there. If it was a guaranteed way to beat the casino, do you really think someone would post it on a public website for free?*

15

Light and shade

If you want to play better poker, play less and play hard. Most of the time, don't play at all.

The classic problem for weak poker players: how many hands should I play, and how many should I fold?

Fact is, most of us take part in far too many hands just because we're sitting at the table, betting the minimum and hanging in when we have little chance of winning. Don't 'limp in', as poker players call it. Bet strong or fold – get some light and shade into your play.

Just as too many punters bet too often on mediocre odds, most of us play too many poker hands in the hope of getting the right cards, when the statistics say that those cards are unlikely to come. This is called 'loose' play, but it's rarely the optimum strategy.

By contrast, a 'tight-aggressive' strategy means that you only enter the pot when you have the cards to raise; you like to raise rather than call; and when your hand's not strong, you fold with no regrets and wait for the next opportunity. Aggression

Here's an idea for you...

This strategy isn't a secret: every basic poker strategy book tells you to do it. But few of us study intelligently, or if we study we browse for five minutes and then go off to play, hoping to learn by experience. The result: we get beaten repeatedly. Read those strategy books and follow the advice to the letter.

like this takes nerve, but it's an exciting way to play; and because you're not leaking 50 chips here and 100 chips there, when you come to take action, you have the stack with which to do it.

How many hands is it appropriate to play? There's no set answer, but the pros will tell you that when there are a lot of players at the table, there are relatively few hole cards that you would play every time. A-A, A-K, A-Q and K-Q, sure. A high pair, fine. But there are lots of cards that can get you into trouble. If you have Q-T, and you enter strongly, you might end up with two other callers. You get another queen on the flop, and you bet strongly. But if you don't improve, and the turn or the river brings either a K or an A, you can assume at least one of your opponents has K-K or A-A. Similarly, a low pair is only good if you make trips on the flop, because after the flop it's pretty likely someone has a pair that beats yours.

So a tight player might play only one in seven hands. A 'rock' – an extremely tight player – might play one in ten. Next time you're playing online, click on the 'statistics' box to see how many hands you are playing. It's a good bet you're playing twice as many hands as a rock.

The second part of being tight-aggressive is the ability to bet to best effect. Always ask yourself what you want to achieve through your bet and adjust your strategy to make that happen. If you're only entering with strong hands, don't put in the minimum – raise it to two or three times the minimum. This might make players with mediocre hands fold – depriving you of their money – but you don't have to face the danger that they fluke a card on the flop, and can suddenly start raising their bets. When I started to play, one of the biggest losses I faced was when I was playing in a cash game for higher stakes than I was accustomed to, and had fallen into the trap of being far too passive. I had A-A in the hole, and the flop came 2-4-10, three different suits. The turn was a 7. The river was a 2. I had gone all in against one opponent, only to discover he was holding 7-2 off suit.

At first I raged because he had hung in with the weakest starting hand possible, but then I realised it was entirely my fault. He was the big blind and I didn't raise pre-flop like I should have, so it was free for him to play. If I had raised, he would have folded immediately. I didn't raise enough after the flop, and having made low pair, I gave him the chance to call when, again, I should have raised him strongly.

But aggression in poker isn't about constantly raising with any card. It's about choosing your moment and betting big when the odds are in your favour. It's about walking away (not literally) from pretty, but usually useless, hands (an ace with a low kicker, for example). It's also about being feared at the table, getting respect from other players, and more practically it's about making sure that you clear out the opposition before the flop.

'There is more security in the **adventurous and exciting, for in movement there is life, and in change there is power.'**
ALAN COHEN, business writer

Defining idea...

If you play online and try a small-stakes sit-and-go (a mini tournament), at any table of ten players, at least eight will play too many hands. At very small stakes an intelligent gambler can usually get down to the final three or four – where you can expect to play with weaker hands – simply by folding every weak hand and raising every strong one. Next time you play online, take note of the 'boring' players who fold, fold and fold again. Chances are, they'll still be there when the flashy players have busted out.

It's the joy of poker that there are many winning strategies, but unless you can play this type of poker you'll never be able to dominate weak players effectively. When they catch on to your method, you will find that many 'calling stations' will start folding their weak bets against your raises, whatever your cards. This is free money, and we all approve of that.

Q   Should I always play like this?

A   You do need to mix up your styles sometimes. The poker saying is that you play loose in a tight game and tight in a loose game. This makes sense: in a tight game, the other players will be happy to fold when you bet, so you can accumulate without ever having to test your cards. In a loose game, you will have plenty of action whenever you raise, so you can limit your bets to hands where you have the best chance of winning.

Q   What if good cards never come?

A   When you dry up, you might not play a card for 45 minutes. Boredom is your enemy, so use the time to study the other players. When you have late position, maybe try to steal a pot with a strong opening raise. But don't suddenly start playing poor hands. Have the courage to wait.

Q   Some players commit all their chips whenever they have a good hand. Is this what you mean?

A   Not at all. Often a smaller raise will have better effect. You want to extract as much from the other players before they lose, so often going all in is poor value: everyone immediately folds, or someone calls you because they know they have a stronger hand. Remember, it's not how many hands you win – it's how much you win.

How did it go?

69

16

Going on tilt

When we lose our discipline and start throwing our money around, we need to get a grip. It's usually much quicker to lose money in a casino than it is to win it.

Everybody goes 'on tilt' at one time when they're at a casino. When it happens it's time to remember our code of the smart gambler and regain control. If you don't, you're giving your money away.

The term comes from the old pinball machines, which used to shut down when they were rocked, flashing 'TILT'. In the casino it happens to even the sanest of gamblers when something upsets them.

Sometimes it's a loss when you thought you were going to win – an incompetent poker opponent flukes a card and wins half your stack, for example. Sometimes it's a player – someone who makes fun of you for losing, or who gets in your way. Sometimes it can be a lost opportunity – another punter leaning over the roulette table

Here's an idea for you... **Going on tilt happens to winners too. When you snag a big win, get a great pot or are 'on a roll', you can lose discipline just like when you get beaten. You start to raise your bets, you feel invulnerable – at exactly the time you are most likely to lose heavily. Watch how people who are winning change their strategy and, if you can, take advantage of it.**

stops you picking your number on precisely the spin when the number comes up. And sometimes it's just outrageous back luck – a succession of seven or eight losing hands at high stakes blackjack.

What do you do? For too many of us, the reaction is that our blood boils and reason goes out of the window (if casinos had any windows, that is) – and so carefully calculated strategies are forgotten. We're on a mission to get 'our' money back. We start to bet into mediocre poker hands, and when the guy that annoys us raises, we re-raise him right back just to show him a lesson. We double our roulette bets, lose concentration and play hunches.

And very quickly, we lose the rest of our stack. At best, we're playing well below our potential, and playing too much – breaking two more of our rules. At worst, the guy who was riling us has us in the palm of his hand. He'll carry on doing it until we give him everything we have. We wake up in the morning with nothing but remorse, thinking 'Idiot!'

Avoid this at all costs. Everyone has emotions; the pot goes to those of us who can channel them positively. Occasionally, you need a helping hand. Plan a ritual for times when you feel like you're about to tilt. In a casino, get up and walk away, or sit out a predetermined number of hands. If you're playing on the Internet, log out and make a cup of tea. At the very least, turn your attention away from whatever has destabilised you – have a conversation, take a deep breath. Sometimes when you are beaten badly at online poker your nemesis will post little insults in the chat window. 'Doh!' or 'Thanks fish!' are two of the nicer things you'll read. But you know – or, at any rate, you will learn – that revenge is a dish best served cold and that you can catch them out later, when you have good cards, rather than in the next hand, when you don't.

There's nothing else to be done. If you are unable to recover from a tilt quickly, or find yourself going on tilt whenever you lose, you really have no business in a casino. But you'll find it easier to cope if you accept that occasional tilting, like losing, is part of life.

Remember the advice of the great poker guru David Sklansky: 'you must consider all the sessions as one big poker game. "Getting even" or "quitting winners" are fallacious concepts.' The same goes for any casino game – in fact, after any losing gamble when you can feel control slipping. It's part of the rise and fall in your fortunes that is the essential feature of gambling.

It's not all bad news. If you can handle your emotions, when you spot someone else who's tilting in a competitive game you'll be able to get into them. Each time you beat people who have lost control you will make them a little bit crazier and a little less likely to make the right decision when you put them under pressure. They'll take it personally, but for you, it's just good business.

'Insults are effective only where emotion is present.'
LEONARD NIMOY playing Mr Spock, *Star Trek*

Defining idea...

How did it go?

Q **In online poker the chat from other players really gets to me; how can I ignore it?**

A   *Most poker rooms allow you to turn off chat, and sometimes on a table with a noisy idiot, it's a great relief. On the other hand, chat might sometimes be insulting, but don't be over-emotional. If someone who's playing well calls you an idiot, it's probably because you were. After the session is over, analyse what you did wrong.*

Q **If I make a stupid bet, can I get it back?**

A   *In short, no. Certainly not after cards have been dealt, for example. If you think you should have been able to withdraw your bet in time but you were stopped for doing so, ask for a ruling from the pit boss – but accept their ruling and never be rude or aggressive. They'll ban you in a second if you look like you can't control yourself.*

17

World of sports

There is hardly any event, sporting or otherwise, happening anywhere in the world where you can't make a bet.

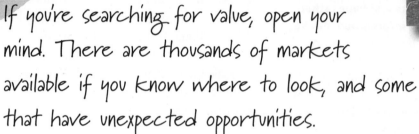

If you're searching for value, open your mind. There are thousands of markets available if you know where to look, and some that have unexpected opportunities.

Bookmakers realised a long time ago that gamblers liked to gamble. This wasn't exactly a revelation, but you have to hand it to them: they have been very creative in offering us ways to satisfy our desire to speculate.

They aren't fools, though. When you see 'special' bets – 'Will snow fall at Christmas?' is one of the all-time favourites – the 'special' isn't usually the price that you are getting. These bets are designed as fun for the casual punter and, as such, are rarely worth our attention.

Here's an idea for you…

People with a deep knowledge of a sport or any sector use their knowledge and contacts to pick up gossip. It's a lot easier to find an edge on lightly traded markets where that gossip is at a premium and prices often represent hype rather than real information. But be careful if you or the source of your information has a contract that forbids you using this knowledge. It's not such a good bet if someone has to look for a new job afterwards.

There are, though, some special bets that might be worth a punt if you think you have expertise, provided you don't blindly follow the crowd that the bets have been set up to attract. Election results are routinely offered as markets. This is a market that becomes quite volatile in the time leading up to the vote, when different pollsters often offer wildly different snapshots of the likely result. The sensationalism of some polls makes punters rush to the bookmaker. Sensationalism makes news, but it usually doesn't make a profit for a punter who believes everything they read today.

Many smaller sports offer markets too and can become distorted by nationalism. If a famous Brit is involved, they attract a disproportionate amount of the money staked because no one has heard of any of the others involved. Bet against the crowd for value.

Also, look globally: while many sports books are becoming 'internationalised' – that is, there's little difference in the odds anywhere in the world – arbitrage opportunities still exist if you bet against the 'home' team for sports where fans rather than unsentimental gamblers bet. A famous example was during the European Championships in 2004 when England played France. Betting on England with a German bookmaker and on France with a British bookmaker was a no-lose bet.

More marginal sports can also have their markets distorted by sentimentality (heroes have lower prices than equally talented villains) or celebrity. On exchanges, for example, you can often find markets with just a few hundred pounds staked. Sometimes you will find a price that's way out of line with what your knowledge and research tells you. The only reason no one else has pounced is because they're all focused on the main markets.

Rarely, you can find an edge of your own. There was a famous betting coup in the late 1980s, where a team of punters discovered that bookmakers were offering odds of up to 500–1 against a hole-in-one being scored at major golf tournaments. The odds of a hole-in-one are about 14,000–1 for any single shot, but for the world's best professionals, playing four rounds each, the real-life odds for an entire tournament were much lower. By carefully spreading bets around so as not to attract attention, the syndicate netted more than £1 million.

It's rare to find these types of opportunities, but sometimes luck intervenes. The Irish bookmaker Paddy Power (www.paddypower.com) has a reputation for offering inventive bets and in 2007 it offered a book on the next high-profile American to be arrested. Clean-living Al Gore was offered at 14–1 and around fifty punters took the action. But Paddy Power had to pay out when Al Gore's son, also named Al Gore, was arrested for alleged drug possession.

Mr. Burns: 'Smithers, is it wrong to cheat in order to win a million dollar bet?'
Smithers: 'Yes, sir.'
Mr. Burns: 'Let me rephrase that. Is it wrong if I cheat in order to win a million dollar bet?'

THE SIMPSONS

Defining idea...

How did it go?

Q   Where do I find unusual bets?

A   *Exchanges carry them – often, there will be a dozen ways to bet on one event. Spread betting companies are fabulously inventive, but beware – because the losses can be substantial. Internet bookmakers that are 'challengers' to the status quo are also creative. We mentioned Paddy Power, but Blue Square (www.bluesq.com) is also noted for its weird special bets.*

Q   Isn't it easy to fix these obscure bets?

A   *Sadly, yes. For example, a spread bet on when the first no ball will be bowled in a cricket match is vulnerable to manipulation if the players involved are open to corruption. If the match is fixed, all your research and expertise can't help you – so bear this in mind when betting on obscure, lightly traded books.*

18

Texas hold 'em

The variation of poker you will see everywhere takes a few minutes to learn but a lifetime to master: here are some basic tips from the experts to get you going.

Poker, and more specifically the variation called Texas hold 'em, is a game that no intelligent gambler should ignore.

It doesn't matter if you don't play cards or if you've never played it before. For a long time I had only the vaguest idea of the rules and strategies, but I thought it was a game for show-offs and loudmouths. How wrong I was.

If you don't know how to play already, learn to play poker. Not only is it a wonderful game in its own right, with variations and nuances that will take years to learn, and nor is it just a potentially huge source of profit if you have talent; but it also takes all the principles of intelligent gambling and demonstrates them to you every time you play. If you play poker well, you'll be a better gambler in every way.

Here's an idea for you…

For a basic introduction to hold 'em poker, use a CD-ROM simulation-cum-tutorial such as T J Cloutier's *World Class Poker*, or GSP's *Poker Academy*. Rules can be hard to visualise in a book; in a computer simulation, they are much clearer. A good tutorial will help you understand the tactics and provide you with a virtual game against computer-generated players. At first the action whizzes by in a blur – but persevere, and suddenly the beautiful poetry of poker becomes clear.

There's not enough space to explain the rules in detail here, but they aren't hard. All the players are dealt two cards, face down – your 'hole' cards. There's a round of betting, where you can raise (bet more), call (match a previous bet) or fold (throw away your cards). Three community cards are dealt in the middle, called 'the flop'. There's another, similar round of betting. A fourth card ('the turn') is followed by a third round of betting, and a final card ('the river') finishes the betting, after which the players left in make the best five-card hand from the seven available. Hands are ranked by their rarity: three of a kind beats a pair, for example; and three jacks beats three tens.

I'm assuming you know the basic rules in more detail. If not, there are many books and websites that can teach you these rules.

Hold 'em has some special attributes, even compared to other types of poker. The most obvious is that any two cards can win. That is, any combination of hole cards can scoop the pot – although some are much more likely to win than others. As each community card is dealt, the odds change. You could go from an 80–20 favourite to an 80–20 underdog in one card.

Some critics say that poker is a game of chance. The truth is that while every hand has an element of chance in it, you might play hundreds of hands in a single session. Bad luck on one hand is usually far less important than sound decision-making.

Why is this game so good? Because it rewards adherence to all our principles of intelligent gambling.

First, it rewards clear, logical decision-making. It rewards the work that means you can make those decisions – if you know the odds of the cards you want, and you know the size of the bet you're making to win the pot, you can make an informed decision. If you guess, you'll lose.

Second, it favours quality over quantity. You don't have to play a hand if your cards are no good. You can fold at any time and just lose what you have put in the pot. The winners are the players who gamble only when the odds are in their favour.

'Listen, here's the thing. If you can't spot the sucker in the first half hour at the table, then you are the sucker.'
MIKE McDERMOTT
(played by Matt Damon), *Rounders*

Defining idea…

Third, you need self-control. If you can't discipline your play, act on hunches, try to chase losses, play too long or for stakes you can't handle, you will be found out.

Finally, it's fun. Not just run-of-the-mill fun; it is hard to convey the exhilaration and the emotional satisfaction of beating nine opponents to win your first $5 'Sit & Go' – a miniature tournament where you square off against anything from three to 200 others. Your brain feels like someone turned up the electricity supply, your mind is opened to every possibility, your attention is 100% focused. Few pastimes are as skilled, as rewarding or as subtle.

This is partly because of the elegant structure of the game. But let's not underestimate the other great advantage of poker: you play against other people. You're not trying to beat a faceless multinational company (a bookmaker) or a machine designed to give you no chance to win (a casino). You can play in person or online, for small sums or large – but however you do it, poker will reward your skills and find out your weaknesses.

World CEO Entertainment ran a survey of 500 chief executives in 2005: 65% of them said they preferred poker to golf, overwhelmingly because of 'the thrill of winning'. If they can still feel the thrill, so can you.

Q   Is this the same game as stud poker?

A   Yes and no. In stud you are dealt five cards and have one chance to change any number of them, and two rounds of betting. It's the game that cowboys play in old Westerns. It's a great game too, but doesn't have as many twists and turns as hold 'em. Online poker rooms offer stud games.

Q   What's the difference between 'cash' and 'tournament' poker?

A   That's a book in itself, but cash games don't have a beginning or an end – you compete with other players to win their money (or lose yours). Tournaments start with everyone having the same number of chips; players drop out when they lose their stack; the top few places are rewarded with cash prizes. You can make money playing both forms.

Q   Isn't it a game of chance?

A   You can't control poker because every card is random. Rarely you will be guaranteed to have the best hand, known as 'the nuts', but most of the time you're using the betting patterns and demeanour of your opponents to assess their strength against yours, and the chance that when other cards are dealt, that picture will change. It's the potential for huge reverses of fortune that make poker so compelling.

How did
it go?

19

Cheating to win

There's a long and ignoble history of cheating in casinos. Most people daydream about pulling it off, but smart gamblers know they are more likely to be the victim than the thief. Here's how to spot it.

You might consider cheating as just another tactic to maximise your bankroll. In which case, we can't stop you, but heed some warnings.

- *Cheating is difficult to do.* The card skills or technology needed to fix games in your favour are simply out of reach of most of us. If you put this much time into developing sleight of hand skills, you'd probably do as well if you simply practiced your strategy.
- *Cheating is fraud.* Casinos will prosecute cheats if they have evidence. At the very least they will ban you.
- *Cheating is detectable.* In a casino, you're cheating in front of hundreds of people who are trained to spot unusual or suspect behaviour. If they suspect you – even without proof – they are within their rights to simply ask you to leave. They will as well.
- *Cheating doesn't win friends.* Cheating can deny other players what they consider to be 'theirs'. They're not going to like you if they find you out. If you cheat in a home poker game, you deserve to lose your friends. Have the guts to lose legitimately or you'll never improve!

Here's an idea for you...

Collusion in online poker is a small but significant problem. Sometimes two players at the table can tell each other about their cards because they're sitting side-by-side, or because they are using instant messaging. It's hard to stop, although poker rooms have sophisticated pattern-matching to find players who behave in this way (for example, folding a great hand for no obvious reason). If you see examples of collusion, report it, because they are taking your money. The quick way to beat collusion is to get up from the table and find a different game.

So, assuming we're leaving the cheating to other people, what should you watch out for? Dealers who cheat are not unknown in casinos, but all the experts I consulted said they were very rare. In some casinos, it has been known for card 'mechanics' to give an unfair deal – from the bottom, second card from the top, that sort of thing. It's unlikely, but possible.

More worrying is what might happen to you at the hands of your fellow players, specifically at the poker table.

The biggest problem is players who cheat by signalling their hands to each other so they can act in collusion. They might engineer a showdown so that one can double the size of his stack in a tournament, or they might use the information not to bet in hands that they aren't going to win. It's often hard to spot.

Sometimes, players try to see your cards. In Texas hold 'em, keep your hole cards face down on the table and look at them by quickly peering underneath, not by lifting them up and holding them in front of you while the hand is in play.

Small-time cheats 'short the pot', by throwing in a stack of chips that's less than they claim it is. Be suspicious of anyone who 'splashes' the pot, throwing a pile of chips directly in. You should lay out your chips in a neat pile in front of you when you bet. A similar thing occurs in every casino game; here, players try to grab back their wager after the bet or substitute smaller-value chips. If the croupier or dealer isn't in control of his or her table, don't bet at it.

Others try to sneak in late bets on horse race winners. When I worked in a betting shop, punters regularly tried to get on a horse when the race was already off. They'd carry a couple of betting slips for the sprint races, and when the race was half-way through they would try to get the better bet on. Bookies are very strict about accepting money too late and will refuse to honour a late bet: they put a piece of paper called the 'off slip' through the tills at the time a race starts, and bets timed after it will be refunded.

Don't get confused between cheating and sharp practice. Players needling you at the card table, pretending to be drunk or pretending to be a bad player when they're actually really good are just executing clever, and legal, strategies. Advanced statistical techniques such as counting cards in blackjack may get you banned from casinos, but they won't land you in court afterwards. Casinos call it 'fraud' to intimidate you.

If you want to get an edge in a poker game, try acting dumb while making intelligent decisions. People might call you a cheat when you walk off with their money, but this is just intelligent gambling.

> **'I would prefer even to fail with honour than to win by cheating.'**
> SOPHOCLES

Defining idea...

How did it go?

Q   Someone told me that online casinos are fixed.

A   There's no direct evidence and it would be a huge risk for the big-name casinos to fix the games. Some players allege that online poker rooms give better cards to new players to create loyalty; but again, this would be barmy for the integrity of their business. If you're worried, only play at the major sites – many of them use standard software to set up their games supplied by companies such as Playtech, Real Time Gaming or Cyptologic. These companies have statements on their sites about audits that show the true randomness of their cards.

Q   What do I do if I think another player or the dealer is cheating in a casino?

A   If it affects you, call the pit boss or card room manager. But be sure of the rules, and of your facts, as this is a serious accusation.

Q   What will happen if I get caught cheating?

A   In films, they take you out back and beat you up. In real life, it's more likely that they will hustle you out of the casino and ban you. Casinos circulate blacklists of banned players, so afterwards you might find it hard to get in anywhere else.

20

Bet for free

Don't learn to gamble by giving away your money. If you practice for no stakes or small stakes, you can make your newbie mistakes and live to tell the tale.

Betting is a test of your ability to pick a winner in an uncertain future. Money is only the way that you measure your success or failure.

Of course, money is handy for lots of other things too, but if you're measuring your success as an intelligent gambler by whether or not you can pay the rent this month, then maybe your strategy isn't as smart as you think.

Not all of us have monster bankrolls to throw around and one of the problems for the inexperienced bettor is that you have to pay to learn because you lose more often than you win. You get it wrong too often, you wind up in poker games against people more experienced and more skilled than you, and you make rash, impulsive bets that wipe out your winnings.

Learning any new skill, whether it's riding a bike, diving off the high board or betting on a horse, involves the potential for mild calamity. But we always try and protect ourselves while we learn the ropes. We put L-plates on our cars and stabiliser wheels on our kids' bikes. We don't let a doctor cut us up until they have practised on people who are already dead. So it would be extremely foolish to immediately rush off to a high-stakes table to have a go at gambling. Better to test your ability where you're only paying with your time and self-respect. Bet for free.

Here's an idea for you...

Get into the habit of regularly studying the form or learning a new tactic when you're starting out. Testing it out on the free tables or by betting imaginary sums on matches or races is a great way to fix this week's new skill in your mind. It's also a great way to discard all the stuff that is either too difficult, too time-consuming or too unreliable to help you in the real world.

There are many places to do this. The most obvious is your own sofa. Try reading the form and using your expertise to pick winners in the racing on TV. Having put in the hard work, the comments of the commentators and the movements in the betting market will make more sense. Many people learned poker by playing for matchsticks with their family or at poker nights with their mates when the chips would be counted up and the end of the night and a first, second and third prize would be awarded. As long as everyone plays like they mean it, there's no harm in this.

Online, it's surprisingly easy to bet for free. Most casinos have free tables where you can try out your strategy. There are also many gambling and poker software packages that will teach you how to play or bet by simulating the action, and replaying it if you made a bad choice. Good poker software also offers you a choice of opponents with different characteristics and playing styles.

Free play is best when you have a goal, a strategy and a plan. For example, you might want to double your 'money' in an online poker game and do so by playing only premium hands. You might want to test out your ability at basic blackjack strategy by sticking to it exactly for half an hour. You could test whether poker slots strategy works. You can try to spot two winners a day for a week or try to get your handicap football betting right 70% of the time. When you succeed, reward yourself with a real money experience – as long as you stick to your successful strategy.

Two caveats: this has no value unless you play properly, and even then the value is limited in some games. For example, it's one thing to pick the winner in a horse race, but was it worth a bet with real money? If you only pick odds-on horses, you may succeed a lot of the time, but at those prices, is it good value? So try to also keep an account of how much you would have won or lost. Don't cheat; be honest.

Bear in mind that the size of your stack of chips in poker, blackjack or roulette changes how you play. You must try and convince yourself when you play that you're dealing with a real bankroll. Even so, this can sometimes be impossible unless your opposition plays seriously too.

'A rich man is nothing but a poor man with money.'
W.C. FIELDS

Defining idea...

How did it go?

Q   **Isn't gambling only genuinely exciting when you're using real money?**

A   *For gambling to be gambling, ultimately you have to have the risk that you lose something of value to you – and usually, that's measured by cash. But if you play football, you'll never be a good player unless you train hard. When you study at school, you won't pass exams unless you pass your day-to-day tests. This is no different.*

Q   **I did the same thing for real money as I did in practice and I lost. Why?**

A   *If you're playing poker, players playing on a free table are usually much worse than real money players. If you're playing a game against the house, the real money tables might have a bigger house edge or you might simply have been unlucky for a short time. If your strategy is right, don't get discouraged by one bad session.*

21

Spin to win

Nothing is more exciting than roulette when your number comes up. But it's easy to lose your entire bankroll in seconds. Here are some strategies so you can keep your shirt.

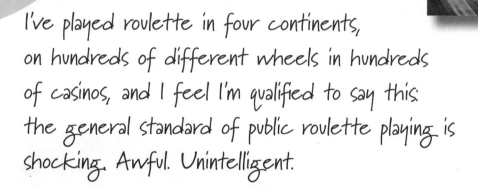

I've played roulette in four continents, on hundreds of different wheels in hundreds of casinos, and I feel I'm qualified to say this: the general standard of public roulette playing is shocking. Awful. Unintelligent.

There may be several reasons for this. First, roulette is a game of chance. There's no skill in choosing red or black, or number 14, or all the even numbers. This means that 'serious' gamblers are to be found in the poker room or on the blackjack table.

Second, roulette is easy to understand, so anyone can have a go – and anyone does. But when a newbie has a go at poker, for example, you can exploit their lack of savvy

Here's an idea for you...

Roulette doesn't have a start or a finish. Every spin is exactly the same; just the punters come and go. It's hypnotic. Before you start, decide a time when you'll finish and bring a limited bankroll to the table. Never start shuttling between the ATM and the roulette table or you'll lose the lot.

by winning their money. In horse racing, unskilled punters helpfully back the losers, keeping the price long on your winning horse. In roulette, they just give more money to the casino; there's nothing for the sharks to bite on.

Third, and relevant to this, it's hard to stop playing. If you've never tried roulette, it's difficult to explain the relaxed flow of the game, the constant cycle of bet, spin and pay. It's the nearest thing that a casino offers to relaxation. So what happens is that you tend to play until you lose all your money. The house edge on a roulette wheel is only a few per cent, but the casino is making five times this at least because so many of us play until we go bust.

Finally, and here's the crucial part: in roulette, the house always, always wins if you play for long enough. You might win one evening, but over time you will lose. There are many crackpot schemes to beat the house at roulette – the most famous/notorious being the Martingale system – but all you need to know is that they don't work.

All I can do is give you the tools to try and ease the pain. I love roulette, I always have. But I don't kid myself for one minute that it's going to make me rich. Put it quite simply: unlike poker, horse racing, share trading or even blackjack under the right conditions, there is never a time when you're playing roulette that on the balance of probability you are more likely to win than to lose. There's no 'hidden value'. After every spin of the wheel, it's the right time to quit.

Why is this? In roulette, the numbers 1 to 36 are arranged around a heavy, horizontally mounted wheel. You bet on one or more of those numbers by placing your coloured chip on a grid on the table with all the numbers drawn on it. If you win, you are paid according to the probability that your choice would comes up. So if a single number comes up, that pays 35–1. If you bet on the odd numbers (there's a place to do this on the table), it pays 1–1. Betting on the 'first third' – numbers 1 to 12 – pays 2–1, and so on. Unfortunately, there's a zero there as well. In the US, there's a double zero. Zero is neither odd nor even (at least in a casino), nor in the first, second or final third. It's not black or red.

That fixes the house edge. You can't win.

So why is it intelligent to play? Look on it as a lesson in chance. It's tempting to think that each spin is part of a wheel's 'story': that is, if red has come up five times, it must comes up once more – or, of course, that it is black's

'In Vegas, I got into a long argument with the man at the roulette wheel over what I considered to be an odd number.'

STEVEN WRIGHT, US comedian

Defining idea…

95

'turn'. If 23 has come up twice in the past ten spins, it doesn't mean that 23 is more or less likely to come up on the next one. Each spin is a new beginning. For the mathematicians among us, roulette is a glorious demonstration of the randomness of the universe, so don't try and chase 'patterns'; although, of course, the randomness means that chasing a pattern will over time be no less profitable than not chasing it.

Second, play cautiously. Some players can't bear to stop betting: for example, you've bet on black. Then you stick an extra chip on your birthday. Then your daughter's birthday. Then on the first third. Then someone who's winning bets on 17, and you can't resist having a bit of their luck, and so on. Players like this win on most spins because they're betting on more than half of the wheel – but they're losing more quickly, because each spin takes a big bankroll. The lesson: don't rush to lose what you have.

Third, respect your bankroll. Different tables have different stakes. If you play with £100 at a table where the minimum outside bet (on sets of number, such as all the reds) is £50, and you lose twice, you're done for the evening unless you visit an ATM. The chance of losing twice in this case is slightly higher than 25%.

And last, learn to walk away. One trick I learned by watching regular players is that if you win early, give a chunk of your profit to someone else or slip it into your pocket. I like to stash the chips equivalent of my bankroll to one side if I get an early win, so I know I'm playing only with the casino's money. Then, effectively, you start again. It takes discipline not to dip into to your profits, but it means that sometimes you will leave the roulette with something, at least.

Q **What's the 'en prison' rule?**

A *In European casinos (and one or two in the US), if you bet on the even money chances, it's not so big a disaster if the ball lands in one of the zeroes. In this case, the croupier takes half your stake, or offers you the chance to go 'en prison'. In this case, your bet has a marker placed on top of it, and stays where it is. Next spin, if you win, you get your bet back. If not, you lose your bet. This lowers the house edge.*

Q **Do some wheels have a string of similar numbers?**

A *All wheels do from time to time, but the wheel has no memory. Patterns are random, even if they don't look it.*

Q **What's the difference between online roulette and the real thing?**

A *Essentially nothing, but online roulette is really boring in my experience. This is mostly because you're playing on your own and also because it's simply not realistic. And it's many times quicker to bet, spin, lose, bet, spin, lose.*

How did it go?

22

Hot for slots

Ding ding ding! It's the sound of someone else hitting the jackpot. Why is it never you? Let's look at pay tables, loose slots and progressive jackpots.

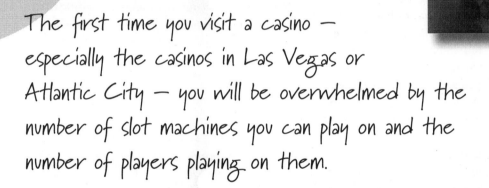

The first time you visit a casino — especially the casinos in Las Vegas or Atlantic City — you will be overwhelmed by the number of slot machines you can play on and the number of players playing on them.

It's remarkable, not least because the casino makes no secret of the fact that the slots can't be beaten. You can play optimum strategy and the only ones with which you will come close are the poker slots.

On the other hand, you might be going to the casino to unwind, and a lot of people find the repetitive action and flashing lights relaxing. Vegas is the US's fastest-growing city for one overwhelming reason: people go there to retire, and many of them enjoy retirement in the sun, playing the slots for a few hours a day. You can scoff, but in the UK we prefer to put old people in a home and make them watch daytime TV. I know which one I'd rather be doing.

Here's an
idea for
you...

If you do play slots, take it easy. Don't be in a hurry. Take a breath before you press the button to spin and don't play more than one machine at a time. Sometimes players have their favourite machines, so if someone has left a jumper or their change bucket on a seat while they go to the loo, indulge them and sit at the next machine along. If you win a big jackpot, take a break and decide whether you want to start feeding it back to the machines. Also, always use a casino loyalty card if you have one – they slot into the machine before you play and, although you might lose all your change, you can still earn enough loyalty points for a drink or a meal afterwards.

Standard casino slot machines are not all the same, but they do have one thing in common: if anyone says a machine is 'due' to pay out or is 'hot', they're talking rubbish. The idea that a slot machine gradually fills with cash until it bursts, showering you with money, doesn't square with the fact that they are computerised. They pay out, by chance, according to a randomised schedule programmed by their makers. And even a huge win doesn't save much space. I once won $600 on a casino slot. It was good fun, but it's amazing how small a pile of quarters worth $600 is.

On slots there's always a tension between frequency and payback. Frequency is how often it pays out and payback is how much it gives you when it does. For example, a machine that pays out if you win on any of the three lines visible, or the diagonals, will pay small sums relatively often. Video poker games pay small sums often. Big jackpot slots pay less often.

There is some technical slot machine jargon terms that's good to know so that you can (probably) lose your money in the way you have decided suits your bankroll. Large casinos commonly offer 'progressive' slots. These are machines where a proportion of the payout is held back for a massive jackpot that builds slowly and is usually shown on a screen above the slot machines. It's like the lottery: we like to play because we want the life-changing prize and are happy to give up some of today's winnings for it. Progressive slots can stand alone, be linked inside the casino, or can be 'wide area' – that is, linked across a bunch of casinos, in which case the jackpot can reach millions of dollars.

There's a problem with progressive slots: many of them, unless you are playing for the maximum stake per spin, don't give you a chance of winning the big prize. So you're feeding the jackpot and getting a lower payback, but you'll never win it. On the other hand, play with the maximum number of coins and you can lose very quickly indeed.

The same is true for 'bonus multiplier' machines. Look at the pay table – the little box on the front of a machine that tells you what you get for each type of winning line. Some pay proportionally much higher prizes if you play for 50p a spin instead of 10p (or $1 instead of 25¢). So they may advertise a 98% return, but if you play low stakes, you're not getting anything like 98%.

Slots are 'amusement with prizes' in casino jargon – there's no skill. The exceptions are the poker slots, where you are dealt five 'cards' and select which ones to hold and which to change, like draw poker. The frequency is huge – just under half the time, you win. You get a lot of small payouts when you play poker slots – for example, you should hit three of a kind once every thirteen spins, but it just pays three times your stake. Buy a card in the casino shop that teaches you the optimum strategy and stick to it if you want to narrow the house edge. On the other hand, poker slots don't make big jackpots.

'They are the new breed of slot machine – colourful, fancy, exciting, wonderful ... and deadly.'
FRANK SCOBLETE, gambling author

Defining
idea...

101

It's rare that a product can advertise that it will reliably leave you with less than you came with, but slots ('We pay 98%') do that very successfully. You might not see the point in them as an intelligent gambler; in which case, why not just give 2% of your bankroll to the pensioner sitting on the first stool and go play a game you can win? It will save hours of your time, and at least the money goes through one more pair of hands before the casino gets it.

How did it go?

Q **I hear that fruit machines in British pubs can be manipulated to make them pay out. Is this true?**

A *There are many sites that promise to give you 'secret' combinations and optimum strategy for these machines. Visit www.fruitmachineindex.co.uk. There are so many machines that if you want to try out the hints, you need to target a specific machine. But remember, this type of machine has a strictly regulated maximum payout. All the insider tips in the world won't make you rich.*

Q **What about quiz machines?**

A *This is in the category of 'skills with prizes'. If you are a trivia buff, you can make a small killing on these machines – but the manufacturers are on to you. If you win a couple of times, the skill level goes up. Just a suggestion: a more sociable way to win might be to enter the pub quizzes in your area.*

23

Learn from the masters

Poker justifies its own section in the bookshop these days. But what are the classics? Who should you believe?

Poker has a rich and varied literature, and every serious player at some point takes advantage of the advice that's offered by poker writers.

Just as every famous footballer ends up in a console game, it seems that every pro poker player eventually writes a book – or at least has their name on the front of one.

Most will teach you something that you need to know, but a few will go far beyond that. There are some classics that should be on your bookshelf. You won't read them every day, but they are written accessibly enough that you can go back to them over and over again.

Here's an idea for you...

If you want to mix your education with a bit more fun, read *Big Deal*, Anthony Holden's account of a year spent as a poker professional. It manages to explain the fascination and the essence of poker (something that the how-to guides don't really concern themselves with), as well as the game's social aspect. Along the way, it details many of the rules and tactics that will help, especially in tournaments. Holden has also just produced a follow-up, called – you guessed it – *Bigger Deal*.

The groundbreaking classic for hold 'em poker was written in 1976 by David Sklansky. *Hold 'Em Poker* has an engagingly hokey look, with a picture of some cards and a gun on the front, but inside it's certainly not a cowboy book. Sklansky was trained as an actuary and he brings his expertise to the game, providing simple, clear explanations of when to bet, how much to bet, when to play and when to fold. He was the first player to rank starting cards in order of strength. The explanation he gives about how to play them, and how that play changes according to the games and your position on the table, takes some beating.

One of the disadvantages of *Hold 'Em Poker* is that it was written when limit poker was the most popular variant of the game. Nowadays, especially online, no limit is more in vogue. It changes the ranking of hands a little, and the betting tactics, but his argument (and it's a good one) is that you shouldn't be sitting down with good no limit players until you have mastered the cause-and-effect of the more statistical limit game.

Sklansky also wrote one of the best books for intermediate players in *The Theory of Poker*, which was published ten years later. It explains in mind-boggling detail the sort of tactics that you can use to take your play up a level. It's written as simply as it can be: I've got a maths degree, and I find it hard to do more than ten pages without having to rest my mind. It's a sort of *Brief History of Time* of the poker world.

The big bumper books of poker are the 700-page *Super System* and *Super System 2*, both by Doyle Brunson. The former looks like is was put together on a kitchen table. The sequel tidies everything up, updates it and adds contributions from many of the greatest players of all time. If you want to know how to play optimum strategy on seven-card stud high-low eight-or-better, there are fifty-four pages of it in here – which I have to admit I haven't quite got to yet.

I've also enjoyed *Improve Your Poker* by Bob Ciaffone and *Internet Texas Hold 'Em: Winning Strategies from an Internet Pro* by Matthew Hilger. Note, though, that when you look at a lot of poker books, you quickly realise that there's a big overlap between the information they offer you. As long as you start to pick up these basic principles, it hardly matters who the author is – you're going to improve.

Be warned, though: there are no short cuts to success. You're in a competitive field, where serious players devote several hours a day to honing their strategies. The most useful way to read books like these is to concentrate on one section at a time. Discover what's wrong with your betting strategy or your understanding of position and concentrate on squeezing every last drop of advantage from that for a few weeks. Then move on to your play on the flop or how to read hands. At every stage you can measure the result in how your play improves.

'Depend on the rabbit's foot if you will, but remember it didn't work for the rabbit.'
R.E. SHAY

Defining idea...

105

How did it go?

Q There are lots of websites offering advice. Should I use them?

A *Mostly, yes. They have two advantages: the tips from the well-qualified columnists are short and snappy, so you can read one a day – like taking vitamins. And it's free advice. As intelligent gamblers, we like things that are free. The online poker rooms usually have columnists, but a special mention goes to poker publisher Two Plus Two for its website www.twoplustwo.com.*

Q Surely if everyone's read the books, there's no advantage in me reading them too?

A *Reading the books is one thing; putting the advice into practice is quite another. There's the problem that we might not understand, or forget, what the experts are telling us. Even then, poker is a game of skill and strategy. In any situation there are several options, depending on who you are playing, how you play best, the game and your situation. The world's biggest books can't answer all those questions.*

24

Tournament play

Online or offline, playing in a poker tournament can be the most exciting way to gamble there is.

Poker is a great game for sitting and winning money. But to win big, you need to start with a large bankroll or to spend a long time working your way up to one.

Sometimes you want to take part in something where you can come out on top – a game with a beginning and an end. There is no shortage of poker tournaments where you can get this feeling. Every type of game and every type of player is represented, so you have a chance to win at lower levels before you advance. You don't have to start off in the World Series of Poker, but it's a good place to finish if you get there.

Most of us will start in what are known as 'Sit & Gos' on the Internet. These are mini-tournaments where you pay a small entry fee and once the number of players has matched the number of available seats, you're off. Part of the entry fee is recycled as a series of prizes – small Sit & Gos pay the top three, for example, and larger ones can pay the first six, eight or ten places. You'll see what the prize fund is before you start. As each player goes bust, the tension gradually rises as to the

Here's an idea for you...

It's a sweet thrill to win even a one-table Sit & Go, but this is many times better when you beat a hundred others to the win. This, however, will take time. On the Internet, where play is fast, it will take a couple of hours – and in real life possibly much longer. Don't miss out on your prize because you only put aside one hour and you have cinema tickets. Have the confidence to budget the time to win the whole thing.

blinds. When it starts to cost 20% of your stack just to pay the blind to hang on in the game, the pressure's on to make a move.

When you play, remember that you can't win a tournament in the first five minutes – but you can lose it. Some players, especially on the Internet, try to steal a few chips at the beginning with reckless raises and attempts to steal pots by going all in on the first hand. No one wants to bust out, so few people will call. But it's an all-or-nothing strategy that works better when the entry fee is $1 than when it's $1000, and if another player has the nuts, you don't have a Plan B.

More sensible players play tight in the early stages, trying to identify the strategies of the players around them. It's good to play only the premium hands you are dealt, whenever they come up. You will pick up reliable pots here and there, trading on the mistakes of others, and suddenly find that half the players have busted out before you've had to do anything more than the obvious. Use late position (when you bet last) on the table to control the game and don't expose yourself when you are in early position (betting first).

If you do manage to win a big pot early, this is a big advantage. You can use it to be the bully at the table. If you have 5000 chips and you're against a player with 800, you can raise by 500 knowing that it's a small part of your stack but most of his. By calling, he's effectively saying that in the next round of betting, he's all in, and he will happily fold so he can fight another day. You can also play loosely before the flop – betting strongly with mediocre cards. Sometimes they will hit and you win a surprise pot, crushing the opposition. Sometimes they will intimidate other players, who don't want to take you on, and sometimes you won't hit anything on the flop – you can fold and still be chip leader.

Sometimes in a tournament you won't get good cards for a long time. Don't panic. It matters most that you're there when the good cards come – players sometimes go from last to first in a few hands. Don't start playing bad hands or you'll bust out in dribs and drabs, the least satisfying way to go. You can survive without playing for a long time. The people who drop out are overwhelmingly the people who played, and played badly.

If, in the later stages, you have few chips and the blinds are high, you need to think about making a move with a lesser hand. If you have been playing tightly, this can have an effect even if you don't have the cards: when you start to bet, the other players run away. At this time, especially when you're close to busting, you may need to go all in repeatedly. You have to take this risk. If you get great cards when you've got few chips left to bet with, you're almost dead whatever your hand. You might triple your stack, but you're still miles off the pace.

When you make the final stages, be prepared to make the running and step up your aggression. Many players go into their shells, scared to lose when they are so close to the prizes. You can win repeatedly by challenging their passivity. Also, look for a fight with the players who have mid-sized stacks. The minnows don't want to bust and have little to play with, and the leaders can bully

'I never go looking for a sucker. I look for a champion and make a sucker of him.'
AMARILLO SLIM, professional gambler

Defining idea...

you or blow you off, but an ambitious middle-ranking player who wants to move up like you do will call your bet. Be prepared to lose gloriously and you stand more chance of winning.

How did it go?

Q   In a big tournament you keep moving tables. How can you keep track of players?

A   *You can't. Concentrate on the players immediately around you. Mike Caro, one of the most analytical poker pros, says that 'most of the money you make in your poker-playing career comes from the players one or two seats to your right, and most of the money you lose goes to players one or two seats to your left'. That's because betting is clockwise: players to the right act before you and players to the left can react to what you do.*

Q   How do I get into the big tournaments?

A   *Poker is remarkably meritocratic. The big tournaments have qualifiers if you don't want to pay a huge buy-in. So if you win or place high in a qualifier, you can go to the main show. You might not get very far, but that's an achievement in itself. The qualifiers are advertised all the time when you're playing online, so they are hard to miss.*

25

Know the score

The ability to calculate the odds of winning in Texas hold 'em is the key to your success. Here are a few tips so you know when to make that bet.

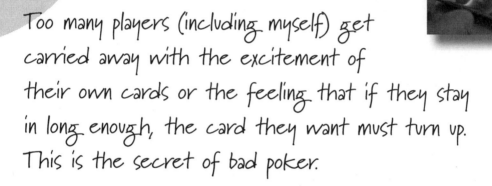

Too many players (including myself) get carried away with the excitement of their own cards or the feeling that if they stay in long enough, the card they want must turn up. This is the secret of bad poker.

Sometimes, you have what's known as 'the nuts' – a hand that, whatever hole cards your opponents have, can't be beaten. If the board has 3-3-3-6-J, and you have the other 3, you have the nuts. If there are four non-consecutive hearts on the board and you hold the ace of hearts, you have a 'nut flush'. In that case, your only decision is how to manage your betting so that the maximum number of players invest the maximum number of chips.

Here's an idea for you...

Practice calculating the odds by dealing yourself two hole cards. If they are cards you would play, deal a flop for yourself. Add up in your mind how many outs you have. Then work out the probability that you would make your hand, using the 'two plus four' rule. Do this in your own time in your own kitchen; when you're playing for real, you will find that your decision-making improves dramatically.

Most of the time, though, you're not going to have this advantage – so you need to make a calculation based on the cards you can see. The easiest part is working out what you have. Then you need to work out what hand you could make and the chances of getting it. Then you have to work out the chances it can be beaten.

Only then will you know if it's worth staying in, investing more or getting out. There's no alternative to knowing the probability of success.

Most poker books will offer you an analysis of probability, and also some ways to make rough calculations. The website www.twodimes.net has an odds calculator for any situation.

It's too difficult for a human to make all the possible calculations in a few seconds, so there are some simple rules of thumb. The most useful – you'll use it every time you see a flop – is 'two plus four'. It states that when there are two cards to come, you find the chance of making your hand by counting up the number of cards that could possibly be dealt (note: exclude cards in your hand or on the board) that would make it, and multiplying by four. It's not completely accurate, but it will tell you if you are 60:40 favourite or 40:60 underdog, and that's a huge difference.

The possible cards to make your hand are called 'outs'. If, for example, you hold 4-5, and the flop comes 3-7-T, the approximate chance of you making your straight is the number of cards that would make it (four 6s), multiplied by four – only about 16%.

There are some stats that for beginners are surprising and can make a huge difference to your betting strategy, especially in 'heads up' (one-on-one) play. It you have A-7 and you're up against A-K, then you're a 70:30 underdog. It's actually better to have 5-6, because if you have A-7 and pair your ace, then so does your opponent. At least with 5-6, you have the chance for two pairs that he or she doesn't have, and the chance of a straight.

Many or us enter a pot because we've got two suited cards. If you have two hole cards of the same suit, you'll complete your flush a sad 7% of the time. Learn some of these probabilities, because you'll face them time and time again.

This maths gets you one third of the way to making a decision. The next step is to imagine what cards your opponents have. Take note of the early betting to make a guess, but don't exclude options because they don't fit your picture of the perfect outcome. In the straight example above, imagine your 6 comes up on the river. You have a straight. You go all in –

'Shallow men believe in luck. Strong men believe in cause and effect.'
RALPH WALDO EMERSON

Defining idea…

113

and maybe you lose, because you forgot to figure the chance that your opponent is holding 8-9, and so just made a higher straight.

Finally, remember that it might have been a good decision to bet in that example; even to call when you're a big underdog. What matters is that your bet return is better than the odds. An example: there's $60 in the pot in a cash game after all the cards have been dealt. Your opponent bets just $20, even though you guess his hole cards mean he will win three times out of four. So if you call, it will cost you $20 if you lose, or you gain $100 if you win. You're getting a 4–1 return on a 3–1 chance. Most times you will lose $20, but it's right to call. This happens regularly in limit games and shows the value of aggressive raises when you think you're ahead – if he had bet $60, your return would have been only 2–1 and you'd have folded.

Remember, poker's not about winning the most hands. It's about winning the most money.

Q   These calculations are impossible!

A   *That's why every poker book lists these sort of statistics for you to learn. You'll also learn through bitter experience of trying to fill a straight, for example.*

Q   This is a stupid game: I was the favourite, I bet big and I lost when my opponent fluked a card on the river.

A   *It happens. It gives you a 'bad beat' story to tell, but the best way to avoid these is to make it uneconomic for good players to stay in the hand by making a call too expensive for them to make – without recklessly endangering your chips.*

Q   I had a strong starting hand and still lost.

A   *Each round changes your position. You have to constantly re-evaluate those odds. If you're holding A-K suited, 9-7-3 unsuited, the flop isn't interesting – but your opponent may be holding 3-3 and he's delighted. You had a monster starting hand, but suddenly you're a massive underdog. Watch the betting and don't be afraid to fold when the cards go against you.*

How did it go?

115

26

Asian handicaps

Thanks to the genius of Asia's gamblers, football betting can be interesting and easy to understand – without being a total rip-off.

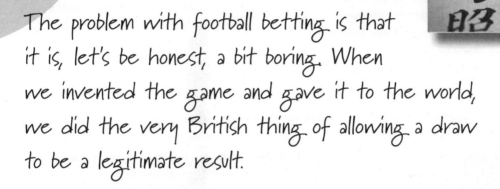

The problem with football betting is that it is, let's be honest, a bit boring. When we invented the game and gave it to the world, we did the very British thing of allowing a draw to be a legitimate result.

In the real world, of course, a draw is perfectly legitimate. It isn't very exciting for gamblers, though. Anyone who has ever bet big with their best mate over who would win the big game, only to experience the anti-climax of a 1–1 draw, will understand.

The other thing about football betting is that the draw can often make the odds for the win look superficially attractive: our eyes are drawn by a 9–4 or a 5–2, which looks good in a closely matched game. It's too easy to ignore the possibility of a draw. Draws make football betting a three-horse race – or a two-horse-and-a-dead-heat race, anyway.

Here's an idea for you… **If you are tempted to bet in-running (during the game), Asian handicaps are easy to read and keep up with without taking your eyes off the match. So if your interest is in football first and betting second, you can put a few quid on quickly without distracting yourself from the match.**

Hence Asian handicaps, which appeared out of the Far East as a clever way to make sure that someone always wins. It achieves this by handicapping one team to produce the nearest thing to an even-chance contest, which the prices reflect. The cleverness, which would make you want to hug the bookies if you weren't worried that they would pick your pocket, is that they usually handicap in fractions of goals, so that it is much less likely that you will experience a get-your-stakes-back draw.

The other useful feature of Asian handicaps is that they are often expressed as a decimal, making it easy for you to calculate the vig and work out your return. And from this, you will see that the margin that the bookies are taking on Asian handicaps is very slim indeed. Compared to fixed-odds football bets, which often verge on being sucker bets, the Asian handicaps offer great value for the discerning football punter.

To explain: imagine that it's the Merseyside derby and Liverpool are looking marginally better, but playing away from home. You want to bet on a Liverpool win. The bet might look like this:

1.5 Everton v Liverpool (½:0) 2.0

The handicap (expressed as '½:0') tells us that for betting purposes, Everton has a half-a-goal start. So if Liverpool win 1-0, you win if you backed them. If it's a draw, you lose, just as you would if Everton wins. In our example, the odds are even money for both, so that it's easy to show what the return would be.

So if you bet £10 on Liverpool and Liverpool win 1–0, you would win £20. If it's a draw, you lose. If Liverpool win 2–0, 2–1 or by any other margin, you win £20.

What could be simpler? Well, there are two small but good wrinkles. Firstly, you will find the handicap expressed as a quarter or three-quarter point. This gives you half the winning bet if you are 'nearly' right. So, for example, if the bet looked like this:

1.5 Everton v Liverpool (¼:0) 2.0

imagine the '¼' as the bet being split in two: half the stake is bet at ½:0 and half with no handicap. If the bet looked like this:

1.5 Everton v Liverpool (¾:0) 2.0

it would mean that half the bet is at ½:0 and half is at 1:0. So if you bet on Liverpool and they win 2–1, you win half your bet and lose half – at these odds, you get your stake back.

And finally, a few bookies muck the whole thing up by offering Asian handicap bets with whole goal differences. That means that the draw is still a possibility: if Everton were given a one-goal handicap and Liverpool won the game by one goal, you would get your stake back and wonder why you bothered.

Nevertheless, these are great little bets. If you fancy your team in a tight match, the Asian handicap rids you of score draw frustration

'We'll bring you the thrill of victory, and the agony of defeat, and because we've got soccer highlights, the sheer pointlessness of a zero–zero tie!'

SPORTS NIGHT

Defining idea...

119

and the quarter-point handicap gives you an intermediate bet. If you want to stop funding the bookies quite so effectively, but don't want to be too careful with your bets, then the margins are only a few per cent. And if you want to compare odds online, Asian handicaps are usually pretty easy to stack up against each other.

The Asian taste for gambling and the ability to innovate have rarely sat so well together.

How did it go?

Q **Which club is the favourite?**

A *However the handicap is expressed, the favourite is the one whose handicap is preceded by a minus and the underdog is preceded by a plus.*

Q **How can I compare Asian handicap odds?**

A *There are several web sites that do this. Try www.asianhandicapodds.com, or search Google for 'compare Asian handicap odds'. As you will see, there isn't a match anywhere in the world that hasn't got an Asian handicap.*

27

Blackjack basics

Blackjack 'basic strategy' and its variants will increase your earnings if you play with discipline.

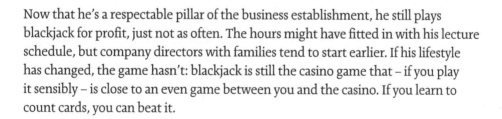

My friend Ken had an unusual job at university. While I was earning less than two quid an hour working at a bookmaker's shop, he played blackjack for a living. So who's the intelligent gambler now then?

Now that he's a respectable pillar of the business establishment, he still plays blackjack for profit, just not as often. The hours might have fitted in with his lecture schedule, but company directors with families tend to start earlier. If his lifestyle has changed, the game hasn't: blackjack is still the casino game that – if you play it sensibly – is close to an even game between you and the casino. If you learn to count cards, you can beat it.

All the fancy tricks in blackjack are useless, though, unless you can play what's called 'basic strategy'. This is a set of rules that governs how you respond to the cards that you and the dealer are dealt. It barely changes over time. Basic strategy takes a few

There are many good blackjack books that will help you learn, but try and find one that explains the differences in strategy that you should use in a UK casino. These are small differences, but the variations in rules will affect your basic strategy slightly. Also, if you're looking on the Internet for online blackjack, go for the best odds, not prettiest graphics.

hours to learn, but it will save you hundreds of pounds a year if you're a regular blackjack player, simply because it educates you in making the right choices.

There's not enough room to explain it in detail here and there are many places on the web or in books where you can find the tables for basic strategy, but it's easy enough to tell you the broad outlines. You total your two cards. The dealer has two cards, only one of which you can see. With those two pieces of information, you decide what to do next.

If you have between 17 and 21, it's simple: the odds are in your favour and you always stand. If you have 11 or less, you will always take another card, but depending on what the dealer has, you will sometimes double your bet. If you have between 12 and 16 you sometimes stand and sometimes hit, but it depends on the dealer's card.

This means doing some surprising things. For example, the dealer has a 7, and you have 16. Almost everyone stands in this position, but basic strategy says that you'll win more often if you hit, even though you will bust two out of three hands.

'Soft' hands (where you have an ace that can count as 1 or 11) are more complex – and don't forget that you will also have the chance to split pairs of cards. Again, basic strategy can be counter-intuitive. Many players split T–T. Never do this; treat it as 20 and stand. Never split 5–5; treat it as hard 10 and hit. Always split 8–8.

It's not the work of a moment but it's also not like an accountancy exam. Even if your memory of basic strategy is sketchy, using any of it is better than using none of it.

The more you know about blackjack, the more fun it is. Try out your basic strategy online – at a free table in an online casino, if you like – and you will discover how well it's working for you. When you feel in control, the experience of sitting at a real casino blackjack table will be much more rewarding for you and your bankroll.

In UK casinos, however, you will find the blackjack rules give the house a bigger edge. The most important aspect of this is that the dealer gets only one card before you act and then plays. If you have doubled and split, and the dealer wins by making blackjack, you lose all your additional bets; in the US, the dealer checks for blackjack at the beginning of play.

Here's some other important differences from casino to casino:

- 'Dealer hits on soft 17.' If you see this, then the house edge has just gone up by 0.3%.
- 'Double down 10–11 only.' You want to be able to double on any total to play basic strategy at its best.
- 'Resplitting is possible.' Say you have split on 8–8, as above, and you get another 8. The best rules allow you to split that too.

But by far the most important one to watch for is 'Blackjack pays 6–5'. Some tables advertise it as if it's a benefit. It isn't. It increases the house edge by a whopping 1.4%. Some tables

'Strategy requires thought, tactics require observation.'
MAX EUWE

Defining idea...

advertise that blackjack pays evens. Don't even go near them. Look for blackjack to pay 3–2, and for the dealer to stand on a soft 17, and you have a game that probably has a house edge of about 0.5% when you play basic strategy. It doesn't take much skill to overturn that edge.

How did it go?

Q   I get offered the chance to buy insurance when the dealer shows an ace. Should I take it?

A   *Insurance pays out for the player if the dealer makes a 'natural' (two-card) blackjack. If you're not an advanced card-counter, don't take it. The house edge on insurance is substantial (it pays 2–1 when the real odds are approximately 2.25–1) and it is only in the player's favour if the deck has a high proportion of 10s in it. So as a rule of thumb: no.*

Q   Some casinos use one deck, some use four, some use six. Is this important?

A   *It will become important when you count cards, but for basic strategy is has little effect – except that you can modify your strategy if you know there are unlikely to be many 10s or aces. Most casinos offering single-deck games, though, give poor payouts and other rules that even things up.*

28

Counting cards

You can beat blackjack if you can count cards. If Dustin Hoffman can do it in *Rain Man*, surely you can too. It sounds too good to be true – so is it?

'No one can count through a six-deck shoe,' says the casino security officer in *Rain Man* as the autistic savant played by Dustin Hoffman wins a pile of money at blackjack for Tom Cruise's character. He's wrong. Lots of people can, with training and discipline. Whether you want to do it is up to you.

The casino's house edge in blackjack can be narrowed using a little strategy. It would only take a little push to remove that edge altogether; this is what counting cards can give you. Blackjack, unlike other casino games, can be beaten.

Counting cards is easier than you think, but don't try it in a casino until you're sure you can pull it off.

Here's an idea for you...

An interesting book on card-counting also happens to be a true story. *Bringing Down the House* by Ben Mezrich is the true story of a group of MIT students who used the Hi-Lo method to win $4 million in Las Vegas during the 1990s. It whips along at a fast pace, telling the story, but also teaching you the elements of Hi-Lo along the way. These are definitely intelligent gamblers.

To count cards, you don't have to know every card and remember it. The 'count' isn't a list of cards. You simply have to keep a figure in your head, and raise or lower it according to the cards that come. The most well-know method, called the 'Hi-Lo', means that for each card of 6 or lower that is dealt to anyone at the table, you add one to your 'running count'. For each card of 10 or above, you subtract one. If there are six decks in the 'shoe' – the plastic box of cards from which the dealer takes cards – the count will return to zero as the full six decks are dealt. In between times it will fluctuate.

When there are more high cards than low cards in the deck, the running count gets high. If you're close to the end of the shoe and the count is high, that's the time to bet high. When there are a disproportionate number of high cards, the dealer will bust more often and you will get more good hands – and will earn more money. When the count goes low, or with a high count early in the shoe, just use the minimum bet. Done correctly, this gives the player a slight edge over the house.

It sounds simple, but there are two big problems when you count. The first is that casinos don't like it. It means they have to give you money, so if they realise what you're doing they might ask you to leave the table. Regular counters get banned. You're not cheating, but the casino doesn't like losing and you're on their turf. In the UK, casinos are less attentive than in the US, but sudden big bets look suspicious. My friend Ken, who played blackjack for a living at university, used to work in a counting team. He used to play basic strategy and signal to another team member by scratching his ear when the count was high. His sidekick would sit at the table as if on a whim and lay down a few big bets – then get up, like any 'lucky' punter, after a few big wins.

The second problem is that it's actually hard to get the hang of it. Practise: using the Hi-Lo, try counting through a pack of cards at home, adjusting the count for each card. At the end of one deck, the count should be zero. It is vital to get this right, because an accurate count is the key to making this work. 'Near enough' means the errors will build up over time and your count is meaningless.

When you can count through the pack in single cards, try doing the same two cards at a time. You will become accustomed to the score of each 'pair', which will speed things up, because you will see other cards dealt in pairs all the time. To survive in a casino you need to be able to count an entire pack accurately in 40 seconds – that's faster than a card a second. Casinos are noisy, distracting places, and if you lose the count, you need to wait for the next shuffle.

A simpler but less effective idea is the '5 count'. Because of the way the rewards are set up, the casino has a bigger advantage the more likely you are to be dealt a 5. If you count the 5s coming out of the show, then sometimes nearly all of them are exhausted early. When the 'five count' is high, you can play basic strategy and the casino has little or no edge.

This sounds like hard work. Well, you're right. If you can train yourself to do this for a few weeks without dying of boredom, you're in with a shot when you try it for real. If not, stick to basic strategy.

'Blackjack is the only casino game an amateur can learn to play and at which he can definitely win.'
LAWRENCE REVERE, author of
Playing Blackjack as a Business

Defining idea...

How did it go?

Q   **Is the Hi-Lo the best method?**

A   *It's statistically effective, but there are other card-counting strategies, most of which are broadly similar in their method and return. It has the advantage that it is symmetrical – it will always return to zero as a neutral point – and it is by far the most popular.*

Q   **Can I use card-counting early in the shoe?**

A   *The earlier you are in the shoe, the higher the count has to be to have an effect – because the less statistically significant it is. So divide the score by the number of decks to go. Say the count is +12, but you have three decks of cards left in the shoe. The 'true count' is really +4.*

Q   **They just shuffled the cards in their machine just when the count was getting high. Do I need to start again at zero?**

A   *Yes. Maybe they suspected you were counting cards. If they did, it's an easy way to ruin your scheme.*

Q   **Can I count cards in an Internet game?**

A   *No – it doesn't work. The software 'shuffles' the cards after every hand.*

29

The art of deception

Bluffing and stealing – the ability to deceive your opponent in poker into thinking you have a good hand – is a profitable but over-used tactic.

Everyone loves the idea of the Big Bluff. With no playable cards, you throw in all your chips and your opponent folds a winning hand. But most of us bluff too much, and when we have too much to lose.

David Sklansky, the first of the great poker gurus, is particularly scathing about the amateur player's tendency to bluff when it won't be profitable. 'People who do not play much poker often think that bluffing is the central element of the game', he says.

Bluffing is always a business decision. What matters is that you bluff when the odds of being called on it are longer than the return from the pot. Alternatively, if you

Here's an idea for you... **Practice the simple rule for bluffing: how many times will I succeed and how big will my profit be? How many times will I fail and how big will my losses be? Your notional profit is the size of the pot multiplied by the number of times you think you will succeed. The loss is the size of your bet multiplied by the number of times you fail. But don't think you're getting better value if you make a small bluff, because they're too easy to call. Your opponent will decide that you either have a beatable hand or you're a rotten bluffer and, either way, it's a simple decision to call the bet and take your money.**

think you're being bluffed, you have to factor in the return you will get from calling the bluff, whether your hand will win if you call and whether it will be statistically right to call if there was no bluff.

You also have to remember what went before: some players suddenly come in with a huge bet when their betting earlier in the hand means they can't possibly have strong cards.

An example: in a pot-limit game, the pot is $40. There are two of you left, the river card (the last community card to be turned face-up by the dealer) was innocuous, and you figure your opponent's cards are similar to yours. Suddenly your opponent, who has been limping in on every hand and betting small, bets the pot. You have a $40 call to win an $80 pot – odds of 2–1. His previous betting pattern suggests a weak hand before the river, and the final card is unlikely to have improved the hand. You think in these situations he bluffs half the time – that's an even chance of winning. Call all night and overall you're in profit.

Now imagine you're that player. You know that people have you pegged for a loose, aggressive player who likes to bluff half the time. Play a hand that looks like a bluff, but in which you actually are overwhelmingly favourite to win, and your opponent will call you. This is particularly effective in no-limit games, where your bet may be huge.

This illustrates the importance of your 'table image', especially online. We all have styles we like to play, and clever opponents will work out your style very quickly and work with it. If you like to call small bets but fold big ones, they will keep you in every pot, 'slow playing' you with small raises when they have monster hands, then making you fold at the end with a big bet. If you are a tight player who only defends top cards, then they will steer clear of calling you when you make a big raise, even if it may be a bluff. You can use this to your advantage by creating a false impression. Some clever players sit down at a table, throw money around and make rotten calls and outrageous bluffs. Five minutes later they go all in. You call, they win a big pile of your chips because they had an unbeatable hand all along, and they settle down to playing tight, by-the-book poker with your chips – their real style. You've just been played.

The subject of 'tells' is another part of poker folklore. It's true that some players give away the weakness of their hands by the way they throw in their chips, making jokes when they bet or acting too macho. Online, watch out for out-of-character betting patterns such

'Many occasional players who visit Las Vegas are constantly bluffing ... and they pay very dearly for their foolishness.'

DAVID SKLANSKY, author and professional poker player

Defining idea...

as quick raises from characters who always like to think for a while – that may suggest deception.

In no-limit games, players might suddenly go all in after a flop that you can't imagine would strengthen their hand. Often, the opposite is true. They realise they have committed a lot of cash to the pot, not improved their hand, but tried to frighten you away. A bet like this shouts 'panic' and, if you have the nerve, call it.

Like shoplifting or stealing from your friend's houses, indiscriminate bluffing might make an early profit in the short term but eventually it will cost you much more. Bluffing is often just wrong: you may be up against inexperienced players who don't understand the concept and just call you, oblivious to the drama of the situation. Bad bluffers also regularly try to bluff multiple opponents, which is mathematically crazy. Example: the pot is $80. Your bluff is $40 against one player who will call half the time. Half the time you lose $40, half the time you win $80 – a great bet. But against three players who will call half the time, you will get away with a bluff one eighth of the time ($\frac{1}{2} \times \frac{1}{2} \times \frac{1}{2}$). You will lose $40 seven times and win $80 once. This is not intelligent gambling.

Remember, it's OK to call what you think is a bluff and to lose, as long as you're getting good pot odds. And it's OK to try and bluff and fail, as long as you're getting good odds. If your tactic fails, just file that information and learn a lesson for next time. And if you can't assess those odds, just don't bluff.

Q **How do I stop the guy next to me from bluffing all the time? It's very irritating.**

How did it go?

A *Wait until you have a huge hand and challenge him immediately by re-raising when he raises you. It shows you're not intimidated. Some people 'steal blinds' when they are in late position – that is, they put in a giant opening bet if no one else is betting and try to pick up the small and large blinds that have been paid to the pot. If you suspect this, and you're on the blind, call them immediately. You might lose, but it will show you can't be bullied – and so is probably a good investment if you're there for a long time.*

Q **What type of hand should I bluff with?**

A *Sklansky wrote about the idea of the 'semi-bluff'. That means you don't have the cards at that moment, but you have a fair chance that they will come. So you have two ways to win: making the other players fold to your bluff and getting the cards later if your bluff is called. Add these returns together. Against this, you're making a big bet with a small hand, and those big bets increase the volatility of your stack. There's not one time to bluff – what matters is that it's consistent with your behaviour in earlier hands and earlier in this hand.*

30

Finding a strategy

Smart gamblers find a strategy before they bet and stick to it through thick and thin. If you're going to bet regularly, you need a strategy – preferably a profitable one.

The trouble with reading form is that it only gives you the information that everyone else has.

The bookmakers have it too, meaning that when you come to bet, much of the information that form gives will have already been factored in to the prices you are offered. What you need is a way to extract additional value from the statistics on offer.

You can do this by solid hard work, checking out every horse or every team one by one. This may yield results, but it's a bit like having all your clothes made-to-measure. The search for a strategy is a way of finding a set of criteria that will allow you to bet predictably and repeatedly, and realise a return.

What matters is finding something that influences performance and isn't reflected in the form guide, isn't obvious from a quick read of the form, and isn't usually

Here's an
idea for
you...

Keep an open mind. Consider anything that you can easily look for when picking horses. Some of the best systems are counter-intuitive. For example, some punters suggest that you pay special attention to six-year-old horses, because most six-year-olds are too slow to get anywhere near the places. As this is the case, the reasoning goes, the ones for whom the owners go to the trouble and expense of training must be in a race for a reason. Does this work? Try it and see.

factored into the odds that you're getting. It's not a way to get 100% winners, but it will hopefully get you value – that is, the horse you bet on has a higher chance of winning than the odds suggest. Then all you do is to find every horse that fulfils your criteria, bet on it and bank the money.

Put like that, it seems easy. But with thousands of other punters all looking for a system, there are few avenues that are unexplored. On the other hand, you don't have to be the only person running your strategy – you just have to have an insight that isn't commonly shared.

A good place to start is the Internet. There are hundreds of sites that offer strategies, some free, some you have to pay money for. All of them sound alluring, but there's only one test: do they work? Before you commit real money to a strategy, spend a week or two logging how it would work. Always keep notes: the horses, the prices and what happened. This is true even if you don't bet them.

When you find something that's making a steady return, bet it for real. It's never a sure thing: horses aren't machines and, especially as the season goes on, there are fewer unknowns in a horse's form. Also, if other people have spotted the same thing as you have and bet on it, this will be reflected in the price you get. But still, keep your log.

This log is the key to value. Say 30% of your horses are winning. If you have a log, you can look for something they have in common. It might be that the 10% of horses in your system starting at 10–1 or above offer a better return if you concentrate your big bets on them. It might be that the system works best for a particular race distance or type. If you spot something that might improve your return, then you might be on to something that few other punters have seen. Your system, at that point, is truly your own.

If this is all you do, betting might get a bit boring. Maybe it's best if this type of search for value is a part of your betting activity, a sort of cash cow that means you can apply more creative resources to seeking out other bets. Or you might want to try two or three different systems and see how each one is doing for you. If your system isn't earning a return over a period of a few weeks, however, you might not be getting the value you think. At that time, take a hint – it's time to look elsewhere for the value you like.

If you're looking for examples of betting systems to start with, try some of the free tips at www.flatstats.co.uk. Here's an example: 'On the all weather [tracks] there is a distinct gender bias which prevents fillies and mares winning as often as they should. Form punters will not know about this and will not distinguish between a colt, gelding, filly or mare. It is therefore possible to create systems based on gender on the all weather and gain an edge over the masses who rely on horse racing form.' Simple: you get better value by betting on male horses. Combine that with your form reading to trim your shortlist.

'Waste is worse than loss.'
THOMAS EDISON

Defining idea...

How did it go?

Q **How do I find this information?**

A *You have to do some work. What you can do is perhaps narrow down the pool of horses that you would bet on in the right conditions and then look out for them. Or you can learn to spot the tell-tale line in the form guide – and scanning the morning newspapers will take a matter of seconds.*

Q **If these systems are so profitable, how come they are being published for free on the Internet?**

A *A good question. There are many systems that will get you a large number of winners, but aren't as impressive as they seem. For example, if I told you only to bet on favourites, you'd have a lot of winners but you might not make a profit at the prices you had to accept. That's why keeping your log is the only sure way to spot value.*

31

Multiple bets

What's a 'Lucky 15' and why is it such good value?

When you're in the bookmaker's shop, you'll see a plastic container packed full of specially printed betting slips with exotic names: Yankees, Union Jacks, Round Robins, Heinz, Goliath Flags and so on.

They look confusing, but they're not: and sometimes they can be good value too, if you shop around. These bets are multiple bets. For example, a 'Lucky 15' is a popular way to combine four bets in one slip. Your four selections are combined as single and multiple bets: you have four singles, six doubles (when two horses win), four trebles (three horses all win) and one four-timer. For a double, for example, your winnings from the first race are staked on the second.

A Lucky 15 is actually 15 (4 + 6 + 4 + 1) bets on one slip and costs fifteen times the stake as a result. So a 20p Lucky 15 costs £3.00. Similarly, a Lucky 31 uses five horses and a Lucky 63 uses six – but costs sixty-three times your stake as a result.

Here's an idea for you...

Don't mess around on small-odds bets for this type of slip: you're making too many small-stakes bets to realistically come out with anything useful. You get the best return from a bet like a Lucky 15 if most or all of your bets are at medium or long odds. That's because while you're unlikely to have more than one winner, you'll get double the odds.

When you're in the betting shop, check out the slips to see how many bets each one represents and what type of bet. If you're in doubt, ask the manager of the shop, who will explain which one is which.

These bets are fun to do, but there are a couple of dangers with them. The first is that many combination bets don't include singles. For example, a Yankee is 11 bets based on four selections: six doubles, four trebles and a four-timer. If one horse wins, you don't win anything. It's worth comparing what you got from your combination bet compared to what you would have made backing your selections at level stakes – that is, dividing the investment you make in the Yankee into four and simply backing each horse to win. If, on your selections, level stakes is better, the Yankee's just a funny name. Don't use multiple bets if you're just diluting your stake.

Also, multiple bets increase the bookmaker's margin. In two races where the overround is 10%, the overround margin on the double is $1.1 \times 1.1 - 1.0 = 0.21$, or 21%. Look for bookmakers with low overrounds if you're going to be betting multiples like this regularly. It also encourages you to make bets that you wouldn't otherwise make. If you picked five horses independently, it's unlikely that you would want to bet every treble or four-timer.

The good part is that bookmakers offer bonuses on many of these bets. The standard for a 'Lucky' bet is that if you have only one winner, you get double the odds. So a single 7–1 winner means you get 14–1 on your bet and covers your costs. Different bookies offer escalating bonuses on these special bets. Compare what's on offer before committing your money.

Many serious punters don't take these special bets seriously; the overrounds on multiples are simply not the best value available when you look at the return, they say, so why bother? In many cases they are right: if you have four horses that you think offer outstanding value on one day, then a Lucky 15 is fun. But there's no need to go fishing around in the dregs for a bet to make up a Lucky 15 – you're just giving away stake money that could have been concentrated on the horses that you would have bet anyway. On the other hand, if you have four, five or six horses to bet and you would have bet them in combinations anyway, you can look on the bonuses as ways to add additional value.

'Part of the $10 million I spent on gambling, part on booze and part on women. The rest I spent foolishly.'

GEORGE RAFT

Defining idea...

How did it go?

Q   How can I work out the return I will get?

A   *There are several return calculators for these types of bet online. The one at www.free-bet-calculator.co.uk is comprehensive and can also be a useful way to find out exactly what the bets with odd names are made of.*

Q   Can I bet these multiples each way?

A   *You can, but it's not simple. A 10p each way Lucky 15 is 20p × 15 bets, or £3.00. But to make it worthwhile, it's usually best to add that it is 'equally divided' – that is, that your winnings are divided equally on the win and place bets for the next horse to run. Otherwise, the win half and the place half are treated separately as win-to-win and place-to-place, as if they were two Lucky 15s: one to win, and one to place.*

32

Drink in, money out

If you want to thrive at poker, stay off the sauce. Conversely, if you want to make money, play against drunk people. They might not even remember who beat them.

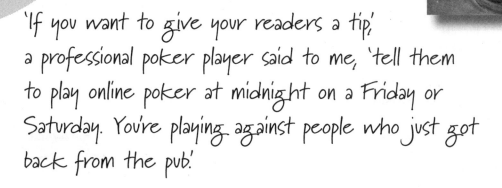

'If you want to give your readers a tip,' a professional poker player said to me, 'tell them to play online poker at midnight on a Friday or Saturday. You're playing against people who just got back from the pub.'

Nothing makes you enjoy poker more than a few drinks on the side. And then a few more, and then some more after that. It's exciting, it's a great buzz, you feel like you could with the poker World Series without really trying. That's why drunk people are easier marks for intelligent gamblers.

Let's look at the flaws in the strategy of playing-while-drunk. Alcohol lowers your inhibitions, so you're more likely to drop in somewhere where you wouldn't nor-

Here's an idea for you...

Obnoxious drunks love to lecture you. If you're online, they'll type random abuse into the chat box, proving that drink and punctuation don't mix either. In the casino, they'll try to rile you with smart backchat, especially when they steal a lucky pot and decide to lecture you on their foolproof strategy. Don't lose your cool and abuse them in return. As my professional poker confidante advises: 'These people are giving you their money. You don't insult your customers.' Stay cool and play the percentages. They'll eventually donate their bankrolls to you in compensation.

mally play – for example a $5 or $10 no limit cash game, when you normally play 25¢ or 50¢. This, you tell yourself, is Your Big Night. The trouble is that high-stakes players are normally better players.

Booze also impairs your judgement of reality. So every lucky pot you scooped gets replayed in your mind as a masterpiece of careful poker cunning. Every loss is conveniently forgotten and you can convince yourself that your weaknesses don't matter, because your strengths far outweigh them. It also allows you to be impulsive in terribly, terribly unwise ways. You start to get a lucky feeling and throw in all your chips with a mediocre hand. You try and bluff three opponents at once. Why did you do it? Because this is Your Big Night.

And it also changes your personality. The inability to calculate simple odds means you start throwing cash at the problem, constantly raising to frighten your opponents. Initially, you'll scoop a couple of pots as the other players try and work out who the hell you are. Then they work out exactly who you are, and that's when you're in trouble, because every idiotic bet you make will be called.

So, put yourself on the other side of this equation. You're sitting in a casino, and the table is full of slightly excited and very flushed businessmen from a carpet wholesaling conference on a night out. They're very, very drunk. How do you play?

Most likely they will be trying to impress each other with super-aggressive play – folding almost nothing, calling everything, making bluffs that have no logic to them, trying to fill straights or draw flushes against the odds. Your job is match your strengths to their weaknesses.

First point: play by the book. They don't respect the odds, you do. Don't force it by trying to win quickly. It will happen soon enough if you play textbook poker.

Second: play tight. Don't enter a pot unless you have a strong hand. Because they're going to play everything for high stakes, sooner or later they will hit the cards they want. If your hand is flaky, then they will take your carefully earned chips. Bad players get lucky exactly as often as good players.

Third: when you play a good hand, play aggressively. They will call everything, so raise them. When the odds are in your favour, challenge them. Pretend your cards are weak: look like you're not confident and they will raise you back out of macho bravado. Keep your nerve and expect one or two reverses, but not that many. Then when your stack is big enough, you don't need to worry about getting busted when someone goes all in and flukes a card, so you can call with confidence when the odds are in your favour.

'In every bet, there's a fool and a thief.'

Proverb

Defining idea...

Finally: don't try to bluff. Drunk people won't understand what you're doing. They are far more likely to call your bluff, because that's what alcohol does.

Casinos don't do anything for free. The reason that they will give you a free drink when you sit down to play is that they understand this principle far better than we ever will. If you want to go out and get hammered, go ahead, it's a free country. Just stay away from the poker table.

How did it go?

Q   **Is this a good idea everywhere?**

A   *Remember: if you're playing online poker in the UK on a popular site at 11 p.m. on a Saturday, it's 6 p.m. in New York and 3 p.m. in Los Angeles. These guys are probably pretty sober, so you can't assume anything.*

Q   **Which online sites do you recommend?**

A   *A tournament winner pointed out that Friday and Saturday night can be the toughest nights of the week to play cash on the major sites such as Betfair Poker, Party Poker or Full Tilt, because they run big-money tournaments on these nights and the tournament players will hang around and pick up some cash on the side. Look for sites where part-timers play: online poker rooms attached to sites that are mostly about casino games or sports betting, or sites that people are also using via interactive TV, are much more likely to contain 'fish'.*

33

The search for value

Gambling isn't about expecting to win every time. It's about what punters call value. Here's how you spot this rare commodity.

What is 'value' in gambling terms? In short, it's when the return you would get from a winning bet is higher than the real-world risk you are taking.

Note that value is not a guarantee that you are going to win. Intelligent gamblers take the long view and accept that they will lose much of the time. All that matters is that at the end you have more money than you did at the beginning.

It's this simple idea that most identifiably separates the intelligent gambler from the herd. Most of us spend our time 'picking a winner'. Sometimes, that's a pretty easy task. In a classic race such as the Derby, where a lot of money has been staked and there is a lot of information about the competitors, if a horse is 2–1 on, then the chances are that most of the time it will win.

But for this horse to represent 'value', it would have to win more than two out of three times the race was run. If, for example, you think it would win three times out of four and you are staking £20 every time, then three times your profit would be £10 and once your loss would be £20.

How do you spot value? This is what every serious punter has been trying to do for hundreds of years, so you have some pretty good company. The good news is that the world of gambling is so rich and varied that there are as many betting strategies as there are punters using them. There are, however, some general ideas that follow from principles of intelligent gambling.

The first is to put aside sentiment. The odds that bookmakers offer are determined by the money that has already been staked. Sentimental favourites, as a result, often represent poor value. If the England football team is evenly matched with, let's say, Andorra, then the chances are that England will be at a much lower price than Andorra. Some of that is because English punters have convinced themselves that (in the words of the football cliché) 'England have their name written on the cup this year'. Some comes from punters who feel obliged to bet out of some weird patriotism. If you sense this is a strong trend, bet the other way.

Stop thinking about winners only and look for value in other areas. Because everyone is betting on the winner, then those markets may get relatively settled and there might not

Here's an idea for you…

Not all 'value' bets are the same. Some offer excellent value, so apply more of your bankroll to them. Some offer a slight edge, so don't commit too much to those. If you do your research and stay in control, you'll have an idea not just where to place your bets, but how much to bet as well. Intelligent use of your bankroll increases your edge. It's not intelligent to bet the same every time – in racing parlance 'level stakes'.

be much insight you can bring that hasn't already been factored into the prices on offer by other punters. More obscure markets might offer the value. You can bet on the number of bookings in a football match or the time of the first goal. You can bet on a race as if the favourite wasn't running. You can use the handicap system to back on football or rugby teams at even odds. All of these markets can throw up better value if you have done your research.

You can also find value by reacting first. Betting markets, like stock markets, are volatile and respond to events. A horse that is poor value at 6–1 might be excellent value at the same price if the favourite is withdrawn. Bookmakers will cut their prices as soon as they get any news – probably before you do – but you might be able to pick up a price for a few minutes on an exchange, for example.

Value is also present if there is information that most people don't know. This insider information isn't easy to find. It's why the really big horse racing punters like to watch horses training and why they have many contacts in the racing business. It also skirts the boundaries of legality. You don't bet on your own team, because you can influence the result. It's good value, but you might find it cuts short your sporting career.

The search for value isn't about finding a monster bet – a sure thing at a ridiculous price. If your edge averages 5% and you start by betting £100 a day, five days a week, that's an average return of 25%. Reinvest your weekly return in the next week's bets and every month you would end up with two and a half times your starting bankroll. That's very unlikely to happen, but it's an example of how a consistent edge in value applied to your bankroll has a huge long-term effect.

'The race is not always to the swift, nor the battle to the strong, but that's the way to bet.'

DAMON RUNYON

Defining idea...

149

How did it go?

Q   **The form guides in the newspapers pick out the best horses. Surely they are the best value?**

A   *Not usually, because everyone else can read the same form guide, Most of us glaze over, and just look at which horses have been picked out at the bottom. By applying a system, or weighting some aspects of the form, or by eliminating sure losers, you might be able to reach an independent conclusion.*

Q   **Is there always value?**

A   *No. Sometimes the bookmakers have a huge margin on a race or a sport, and so it's tough to find any price that represents value. Sometimes there might not be any significant insight that hasn't been factored into the price. And sometimes we simply don't know enough about what will happen – for example, an early-season horse race where the runners are making a first or second appearance. In that case by all means watch but don't bet.*

34

Spread betting

Danger! Almost unlimited losses ... but also the chance for spectacular profits if you have the nerve and the insight to bet like a trader.

If you want to try spread betting, be warned: you can lose your shirt, and your trousers and shoes too. Of course, there's also the potential for huge wins.

Spread betting combines betting with the idea of playing the financial markets. If you think you have an edge on the bookmakers, it's one of the most effective ways to profit from it.

Here's how it works: you have looked at the statistics and you think that the first goal in a football match will be scored early. Maybe there's a pattern of one of the teams letting in sloppy goals or perhaps you've just heard that the centre-half has failed a fitness test.

This is one of the classic spread bets: when you look, the 'spread' is thirty-three to thirty-five minutes. This means that the spread betting company believes that the first goal will be scored between the thirty-third and thirty-fifth minute. If you think

Here's an idea for you...

Spread betting gets confusing sometimes because of the trader terminology. If you go to www.bethilo.com, a site run by Sporting Index (which has 70% of the UK spread betting market), then lots of the jargon is stripped out and the minimum bets are small. The site talks about going 'high' or 'low' instead, and shows your maximum profit and loss when you make a bet. It's essentially the same market, but easier to understand, and is a good way to find your feet.

the first goal will go in early, you go low – in spread betting terms, you 'sell' the low figure. If you think that the first goal is going to be scored late, you would 'buy' the high figure.

Here's the risk part: your stake is multiplied by how many minutes either side of your prediction the goal is scored. If you get it right and the first goal goes in on 7 minutes, a £10 stake wins $(33 - 7) \times £10 = £260$. You got a 25–1 return. If the first goal is scored on 28 minutes, you win $(33 - 28) \times £10 = £50$. Still a great return. If, however, the first goal goes in on 88 minutes, you're in a world of trouble and will lose $(88 - 33) \times £10 = £550$.

As you can see, spread betting is not for a conservative punter. It can be an intelligent gamble, though: if you have a strong opinion that you will beat the spread, it will probably offer a much better return on your stake than a traditional bookmaker or a betting exchange. You just have to be prepared – and able – to swallow a big loss if you get it wrong.

Bet with caution when you deal with spread betting. Don't follow hunches. If the quoted prices on the spread look crazy to you, bear in mind that the people offering them have done their research. If you think you can beat the spread, try and come up with a good reason why that would happen – and try even harder to come up with a reason why you might be wrong.

There are more conservative spread bets. For example, if you want to bet on American football, Sporting Index (www.sportingindex.com) allows you to pick three teams. If all three win, SI awards 50 points. If any team scores more than 40 points in the game, the total SI points score is increased by 10 for each team that does. So the maximum total is 80 points and the minimum is 0 points. A typical spread for this bet is 31–34. If you buy at £10, all three teams win and one scores more than 40 points, the score is 60 and your return is $(60 - 34) \times £10 = £260$. There are championship and relegation indices on football: the Premier League winner gets 60 points, the second 40 points, the third 30 points and so on. Arsenal might be offered at 41–44. If you buy at £10 and Arsenal win the Premier League, that's a return of £160, much better than the return from a bookmaker. If Arsenal finish second, though, you lose £40 – and if they slump to fourth, you lose £240.

When even a conservative bet offers a huge downside, you need to be prepared to close or protect your positions early when the spread moves in your favour. Here's how: You bought Arsenal at 28 for a £10 stake, at the beginning of the season when the spread was 25–28. If Arsenal do well and the spread moves to 41–44, you might want to give yourself a bit of insurance by selling Arsenal at £5 a point.

If Arsenal win the Premiership, you win £320 and lose $(60 - 41) \times £5 = £95$ for a net profit of £225. For second place, you win twice over: $(40 - 28) \times £10$ and $(41 - 40) \times £5$ for a total profit £125. Third place nets a profit too, as does fourth. Only when Arsenal slump to fifth do you move into a slight loss. If Arsenal slump to tenth and score no points, you lose £280 on the first bet, but win £205 on the second one, which is a bearable overall loss of £75. Bearable if you're not an Arsenal fan, that is.

'Risk is essential. There is not growth of inspiration in staying within what is safe and comfortable.'

ALEX NOBLE

Defining idea...

The excitement of spread betting is that sometimes a price looks too good to be true – but they are carefully constructed markets where value is as hard to find as ever and the punishment for getting it wrong can wipe out a hard-earned bankroll in a few minutes.

How did it go?

Q   Can you bet the spread on anything?

A   *There are many innovative and interesting markets, but if you want to bet on a particular horse or a football team, spread betting isn't very useful. For example, you can bet on the total winning margin of a horse because that can be expressed as a number, but not the name of the horse.*

Q   Are there any very risky markets?

A   *Yes – lots. For example, the number of runs in a one-day cricket match, which can be anything from 200 to more than 600. If you go low for £10 a run at 480 and 700 runs are scored, you lose a wallet-popping £2200. So always remember: unlike a standard win bet, your potential liability will be many times your stake.*

35

Going to the bookie

Betting shops used to be intimidating places, but now they're desperate to attract as many of us as possible. Here's how to make the most of the incentives on offer at your local shop.

Betting shops have always had the reputation of being seedy places that are off limits to upright men and all women.

That's changed a lot in the last few years, but they can still be intimidating, and now that you can bet from the comfort of your sofa a lot of people prefer to avoid them altogether. There are around 8500 betting shops in the UK and they can still be useful places for the smart gambler to know.

There are two very good reasons to go to a betting shop. First, you can see the races. Television shows only a few race meetings these days, unless you subscribe to a satellite or cable package that includes them (which, if you're really committed, might be money well spent). Second, you can read the form. The first thing you will see when you walk in the door of a bookmaker's shop is that the walls are literally papered with that day's form from the *Racing Post*. One of the first jobs a shop manager has in the morning is to pin this up around the wall, where it sits all day while most punters studiously ignore it. If you want to read the form but don't want to buy the paper, then here's a free way to do it.

Don't drift into a betting shop with no plan, just to see what's on. If you do this, you're one of the punters that contribute to their fat profits. Pick a specific race or races; narrow down your selections before you go. Have an idea of the target price you want before you place your bet. Then, by watching the build-up to the race you can see how your horse is doing, and whether the market is moving in your direction. But always be ready to walk out without placing a bet if there's no value for you.

There are other reasons to visit the shop. If you want to find out prices on obscure events, then the staff behind the counter are happy to look them up for you, and they can also give you advice on how to mark up your betting slip, or what races have 'early prices' – fixed prices offered on the morning of a race to tempt punters into the shop. Because betting shops need to get you in the door, there may also be 'specials' offered only in the shops – for example, a football team that is available at 7–4 to win the league could have a one day 'special' at 11–5. Some shops offer 10% bonuses on winning bets provided you bet with them again or pay bonuses on multiples.

If you have a question, any question, ask at the window where you place a bet. The managers have a lot of knowledge and, especially in busy shops, will welcome the diversion from the ordinary stuff of settling bets.

These are all sound reasons, but when I worked in the shops one of the reasons why many of the regulars came in was to meet their friends. Betting can be a solitary business; reading form, planning a strategy and picking your bets isn't very social, as your significant other might have pointed out to you in the past. When you then place your bet on the Internet and pick up your winnings by having them automatically credited to your account, it means you can gamble without interacting with any other human being. There's a lot of rubbish talked in betting shops (I've found that, usually, the louder the punter, the worse the advice), but some people really know what they're talking about. And even if they don't, sometimes it's just more fun to share your successes and failures with other people.

When I lived in South Manchester, several of the shops I used to work in were also the centre of the trade in stolen goods for the area. Whether or not that's a recommendation for you is up to you to decide.

That's the good news. The bad news is that, as the range of products that betting shops offer has increased, so have the opportunities to waste your money on sucker bets. The odds on unusual bets – such as who will win a reality TV show or whether it'll be a white Christmas – are often terrible. They're geared towards people who are drunk, or who bet for sentimental reasons, rather than a hard-nosed punter like you. Then there is the abomination that is 'virtual racing' – computer-generated races featuring horses and jockeys that aren't real, even though the money you spend backing on them most certainly is. The virtual races are there to cover dull times when there isn't a race on so that punters don't drift away. If you want to bet on something arbitrary, go home and bet on the toss of a coin with your mate. It's a complete waste of time, but then at least you're not paying a bookmaker to waste your time for you.

The shops are now also permitted to install slot machines for people who can't lose their cash fast enough the usual way. If you find that you're wasting money on these, then you're not controlling where you put your bankroll. A betting shop probably isn't a good environment for you. Go home.

'A man's gotta make at least one bet a day, else he could be walking around lucky and never know it.'

JIM JONES

Defining idea...

How did it go?

Q   **I got a tip from this guy in the shop. He's always there, so I reckon he knows what he's talking about.**

A   *He probably reckons he knows, but don't trust confidence – trust analysis. The form's on the wall in front of you, so look at it. Ask him why he fancies his tip. Often you'll find that shop tipsters mumble something about a bloke who knows someone. This is not a reliable basis on which to gamble. If he's a regular, test out a couple of his tips before you give him any credibility.*

Q   **Do different shops offer different prices?**

A   *Just as supermarkets do, so do the betting shops. Most newspapers publish price comparisons, especially before big races, and the bookmakers publish advertisements with their early prices. Like the supermarkets, these differences are usually small, so the money and time you waste driving across town to get 11–2 instead of 5–1 isn't going to make a big difference. The big point of difference might be special offer bets, but while choosing one shop over another may be smart, it isn't going to make your fortune – especially since exchanges will often beat both prices.*

Q   **Those bets they advertise in the window look great!**

A   *Often the prices shown in the window are football multiple bets: 'Man Utd to win 3–0 and Rooney to score first'. They look attractive but usually they are sucker bets, designed to draw in the casual punter who prefers to window shop than check statistics.*

36

Numbers count

Statistics aren't damned lies in the gambling world. You can compile your own or subscribe to a service, but any professional punter knows that there's no substitute for detailed knowledge of the numbers.

A few years ago I interviewed a professional gambler. 'How do you beat the bookmaker?' I asked. 'Do your research,' he said. I asked if there was any other way, because that sounded hard. 'No,' he shrugged. 'That's the only way.'

Doing research doesn't mean you are destined to profit from your bets, but if you're going to try to get a reliable return it's the only way to succeed. It's still not very exciting, but it is easier, because there are now several ways to pay other people for their research.

Horse and dog racing have a long-established industry that compiles and publishes form. But other sports have plenty of statistics, if only you could get your hands on them.

Here's an idea for you...

Why not do some of your own research? It doesn't have to be too arduous. For example, if you're looking at how many runs will be scored in a cricket match, you might decide that a big factor is the time of year; in the early part of the season, the pitches are more difficult, or the bowlers might not like the cold, or the batsmen are out of form. It doesn't take long to look up the scores in the latest edition of *Wisden* to see if there's a trend that isn't reflected in the odds.

There are products available to the professional punter. You'll have to pay for a subscription, but for that subscription you'll get top-quality information. The daddy of all statistics services is Opta Sportsdata (www.optasports-data.com), which compiles the stats that you see in the newspapers about who runs where on the pitch, when teams score and how. It does offer products for gamblers, but it's not a priority – indeed, it earns good money by supplying its products to the bookmakers so that they can make markets. This is especially true of the spread betting

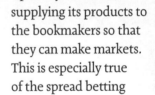

companies, which make markets based on exactly the sort of statistical data that Opta provides.

This creates a problem: you're trying to get one up on the bookmaker by using exactly the sort of data the bookmaker is using, and you're paying for it. What matters is that your research points to an edge over that market; for example, by viewing the data in a different way.

There's at least one website set up specifically to do this: StatsOnSport (www. statsonsport.com) compiles its own data on football, golf, tennis, cricket, F1 and rugby union, and if you are a subscriber it will also give you an analysis and suggest where there is value when you bet that week. On one hand, you're looking at data that isn't exclusive to you, but on the other hand, not many people are serious enough about their betting to want to pay a subscription. Each week it publishes an analysis of where its recommendations paid off and where they didn't. There's also a lot of free content on the site, with a basic analysis of teams that suggests their strengths and weaknesses. It's all done from the punter's perspective, so even the free stuff is a huge help when you're creating a strategy. You'd be mad to ignore it.

If football betting is your thing, there's another smaller-scale site that is definitely worth a look. Football Anorak (www.footbal-lanorak.com) compiles form statistics and has some innovative features. For example, it

'Not everything that can be counted counts; and not everything that counts can be counted.'
GEORGE GALLUP, inventor of the Gallup poll

Defining idea...

compiles a league table of the football teams that give the best return when they are outsiders in the betting, and it lets you create customised form tables. Again, it's free, so it has to be a resource that you use when you're looking for value – even if just to test your intuition.

Searching for the best odds between half a dozen bookmakers has no meaning if the best price you get is 5–1 but your research shows that 6–1 is the minimum price that offers acceptable value. So while there will always be a place for sites such as OddsChecker, unless you're also doing your statistical research, you're checking the price of something that you don't know the true value of – and that's going to compromise your earning potential.

Q   **The team I'm backing has only won once at this ground in the last** **How did** **five games. So am I a fool to back it?** **it go?**

A   *Historical statistics have their limits, especially in football. Three years ago the chances are the team probably had a different manager and mostly different players, as did the other team. One might have been challenging for the title while the other was marooned in mid-table with little to play for. The statistics are never the whole story, and sometimes can pose more questions than they answer, so don't just become a Statto: interpret what you see.*

Q   **There's someone on the radio whose dog picked the winner of the Grand National two years in a row. Should I take the dog's advice?**

A   *Because one thing happened after another doesn't mean they're related. There are hundreds of people in the world who let their dogs pick the winners of horse races. At a guess, this succeeds exactly the number of times that any random method would. In a 30-runner race, if a thousand dogs picked a horse, about 30 would be right. So one in a thousand dogs will pick the winner two years in a row. The dog's not got insight, it has just been selected by chance. Because of the despicable lack of knowledge about how probability works in our society, the dog ends up on the radio.*

163

37

Losers can win

In a sporting event you don't always need to back the winner to win. Many gamblers make good money on second or third places.

Some races have, in betting terms, only one winner. Sometimes one horse, runner or football team is so superior that your fellow punters decide that it's silly to put their money anywhere else.

The odds will reflect this money. That's when the favourite is 'odds-on', reflecting that it has more than a 50% chance of winning in the eyes of the punters. So '2–1 on', less confusingly written as 1–2, means that for every £1 you bet, you win 50p – a total return of £1.50.

Some punters follow this strategy of backing odds-on favourites with large sums of money. They reason that it takes some of the chance out of the betting game. An example is a horse that's a strong favourite because it is faster, stronger and better handicapped than the other horses by a long way. Some random occurrences that

Here's an idea for you…

If you're looking for value in each way betting, concentrate on the bigger races. With 12 runners or more you're getting a quarter of the odds and three or four places, and sometimes bookmakers will offer bonuses – maybe paying an extra place or a third of the odds. If you have an outsider in one of these races, then it's a great time to back it, because there's much better value available than usual.

would spoil the chances of a lesser horse – for example, a slow start or being hampered by other horses – are less likely to affect a strong favourite. The same goes for a rugby team that concedes an early try but goes on to win 52–7.

The disadvantage is that when you come unstuck, you lose big money. Sometimes it's better to focus on how you win by ignoring the favourite.

One of the innovations in the betting market in the last few years has been widespread 'without the favourite' betting. An example is the Christmas Number One in the music singles chart, which in the past few years has been dominated by the winner of *The X Factor*. It's not a very interesting market, because the *X Factor* winner is at a laughably small price following lots of money from occasional punters who don't care if they get evens or 1–8.

So the bookies run a separate book that marks the prices as if the favourite didn't exist. If you back the horse you fancy in this book and if it comes second to the favourite, you still win. If it comes first and beats the favourite, you win as well. It's at a lower price because of this, but often it's a more interesting bet; not least because your research might tell you that there's a standout horse that's not going to win, because another horse is simply a class above.

The other way to bet on a team, horse or a player that is probably not going to win is to take 'each way' odds. An each way bet is effectively two bets: one that your pick wins and one that it comes close to winning. The 'place' half of the bet is offered at reduced odds, which will be made obvious to you when you see the description of the race.

For example, in a handicap with 12 runners, an each way bet pays out for first, second or third at one quarter of the odds. Imagine your horse is at 10–1 and you bet £10 each way. That means you pay out £20. If your horse wins, then you win a bet of £10 at 10–1 plus a bet of £10 at one quarter the odds (5–2) for a total return of £110 + £35 = £145. If it comes second or third, then you get only the place portion of the bet, i.e. £35.

There are two ways to use each way bets to your advantage. The first is for an outsider that you fancy strongly but you think there are one or two classier horses in the field. If your horse is 20–1 or above, you are still getting a good return if it places. This rewards strong horses and game triers, consistent unglamorous runners that tend to get overlooked in the betting.

Or you can use an each way bet as a sort of insurance on shorter-price horses. At 8–1, a horse will pay out well when it wins. But if you have doubts about it – perhaps it lacks stamina in a sprint finish – an each way bet will still see you in profit if it places. Beware, though: in fields of seven horses or less, each way pays only two places, and in fields of between eight and eleven runners, a place pays one-fifth odds, so this becomes less attractive as a strategy.

'Waste is worse than loss.'
THOMAS EDISON

Defining idea...

How did
it go?

Q **During the football World Cup I've seen each way bets offered for the countries, meaning that they have to win the tournament or come second. Is this good value?**

A *Often, it isn't. The way to decide is to think what that team will have to do to reach the final – how many matches it would have to win and the likely odds of winning those matches. In a straight knockout it's usually more profitable to back your player or team in each round, maybe reinvesting some or all of your winnings.*

Q **Is an each way bet the same as a place on the Tote?**

A *When you bet on the course with the Tote, you can back a horse for a place only. The dividend you get is the same if it finishes first or second (or third or fourth for larger fields). It's like an each way bet without the win half of the bet and, being a dividend, you have no control over the odds you get. But it allows you to focus all your money on the place option instead of splitting it in half.*

38

Reading form

The columns of numbers in the newspaper look like gobbledygook. But the better you are at studying form, the more successful your horse racing bets will be.

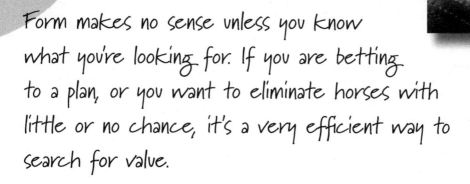

Form makes no sense unless you know what you're looking for. If you are betting to a plan, or you want to eliminate horses with little or no chance, it's a very efficient way to search for value.

Here's a fictitious line from the newspaper:

4 (13) 2473 Tim's Fancy 7 D C BF Vincent Wong 4 9-6 Billy Whizz (4) 88

What's that all about? First, the explanation. Horse number four is drawn in stall 13. On its last race it came third; before that was seventh, before that fourth, and before that second. The horse's name is Tim's Fancy and it has been seven days since its last race. It has previously won at this distance (D) and on this course (C), and last time out was the beaten favourite (BF). The trainer is Vincent Wong, the

Here's an idea for you...

At the bottom of the form guide in the *Racing Post* or on your race card, there will usually be an analysis from an expert of which horses have a good chance. Not surprisingly, the horses that are singled out will attract a lot of punters who prefer to follow the crowd. If you find a horse that is dismissed in the analysis as a no-hoper, then by matching your expertise against theirs you get better value for your selection, because it will probably have a longer price.

horse is four years old and it carries nine stone six in the handicap. The jockey is Billy Whizz, who is claiming four pounds (meaning the actual weight it carries is 9-2, and its rating (a calculation of its prospective future form made from adding together several criteria) is 88.

So that's an explanation of what the numbers in a form line represent in every race card, but what do they mean? To most of us, most of the time, they mean nothing. After all, translating this into a full picture of the horse's chance by trying to build a sort of photofit would take all day. You can try to do that if you like – the rating at the end is one experienced expert's view – but it will take a lot of trial and error.

A more practical way to use form is to match the horses to your betting strategy. To do this, you need a strategy, and some evidence that your strategy can pay off for you. This happens over days and weeks: make your bets but note down why you made those bets, what happened and, if you are beaten, what the form of the horse was that beat you. This has two benefits. When you need to modify your strategy (or abandon it), it gives you the evidence and suggests what sorts of horses are beating your selections. It also makes reading form second nature and speeds up the tedious process of acquiring the knowledge that you need when you want to bet.

If you're time-limited and an occasional punter – as most of us are – reading form becomes more valuable, not less. In that case, a simple system will suit you best. An example: some punters like to bet on beaten favourites, because they believe that the market punishes beaten favourites disproportionately – perhaps because if a horse has let you down, you are emotionally biased against it. In that case, look for the horse with 'BF' next to its name and check the price.

Other punters follow a local trainer or horses of a certain age that are lightly handicapped. The handicap exists to give every horse an equal chance: based on its previous results, the jockeys have to carry weights in the saddle. The more successful the horse, the more weight it must carry.

The form is a basic guide and it helps you make a basic assessment of value, but always remember that value isn't just about the chance of winning – it's about the price you are offered and any statistical trend you have spotted that isn't reflected in the form.

In the end, form can be your basic guide, or a way to pre-select horses that you're going to take a longer look at. Whichever way you use it, by all means use it. Form is free information, so we'd be foolish not to.

'I have but one lamp by which my feet are guided, and that is the lamp of experience. I know no way of judging of the future but by the past.'
EDWARD GIBBON, English historian

Defining idea…

171

How did it go?

Q   Where can I find form guides online?

A   *The most comprehensive guide is at www.racingpost.co.uk. You will need to register and, to get hold of the form guide, you will have to pay a small charge – 20p each time. This soon mounts up, so it might be better to do it the old-fashioned way and buy a newspaper. Or, of course, you could go to a betting shop, where it's pinned up on the wall.*

Q   Why is a horse that came seventh in its last race the favourite today?

A   *Form doesn't tell you some of the most important things you need to know. For example, you don't know what the standard was of the last race, or what conditions it was run in – two very important factors. Finding the answers to these questions will help you find an edge or avoid a bad bet.*

39

Greening out

When you bet on the exchanges, you don't have to wait for the final whistle to make a profit. Many pros have made their profits long before the final whistle or the finish line.

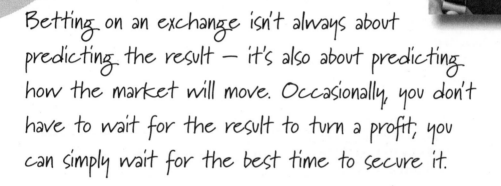

Betting on an exchange isn't always about predicting the result — it's also about predicting how the market will move. Occasionally, you don't have to wait for the result to turn a profit; you can simply wait for the best time to secure it.

This is simply city trading translated to sport. It's second nature if you're accustomed to playing the stock market, but for the rest of us it takes some getting used to. Do it well, though, and you can achieve what's known on the exchanges as 'greening out'. That's because when you look at the event odds on Betfair, there's a number in front of each participant that shows how much you stand to win if that horse or team wins. A green number is a profit and a red number is a loss. It is possible to get a full screen of green numbers – you can't lose.

Here's how it works: a long time before the event, you find odds offered of 50.0 on your fancied runner. You speculate £10, a return of £500 if you win. But let's assume that a horse with this return is unlikely to win.

In the following weeks, the horse shows good form, or its rivals show poor form, or the weather favours it, or all three. When you check again, the return is 10.5 to bet and 10.0 to lay. You can get excited that its chances are much better and let your bet ride – or you can be an intelligent gambler and make it a no-lose bet.

The important thing is that, at 10.0, the market still thinks that your horse will lose 90% of the time – and so nine times out of ten your prescience will have no financial value. Losing £10 at 50.0 or £10 at 10.0 still means losing £10. But by laying the horse – gambling that it will lose – you can 'green out'.

Here's an idea for you...

If you find it tough to work out the stakes and returns, there's simple free software at www.arbcruncher.com. It offers several types of calculation and you can download it as a toolbar or open it as a pop-up window. It's often hard to work out what stake will optimise your arbitrage return: some commercial software will do this for you, such as *Bet-IE* at www.bettingprofitsoftware. com, but it costs £97 to download.

Lay the horse at £30. If the horse wins, you have profited £490 on the bet, but lost £300 on the lay. You make a profit of £190. If the horse loses, you lose your £10 stake on the bet but make £30 on the lay – a profit of £20. Nine times out of ten, you profit by £20. The tenth time you make £190.

These arbitrage opportunities will arise surprisingly often, and taking advantage of them will rely on your ruthlessness. It's tough to give up on the dream of winning hundreds of pounds for a secure return of a few pounds, but when the market moves like this you're being given the chance to profit whatever happens – and it's smart to take advantage.

You don't have to restrict yourself to the exchanges for this, but it's harder to do at a bookmaker because you can't lay a horse or a team – so really, the only opportunities you get are in small fields or head-to-heads, such as a rugby game or a snooker final. In that case, you will need to back each competitor to win at different times to ensure a result. An example would be if one team was offered at 2–1 and one at 5–2 on. You bet £20 on the 5–2 on favourite for a profit of £8. Then the other team loses its star player, and goes out to 4–1. Invest £6 on the outsider. If it wins, you have a profit of £24 and a loss of £20. If the favourite wins, you have a profit of £8 and a loss of £6.

This is called 'Dutching', and in horse-racing it takes a lot of skill and experience to do it. Many serious punters, however, calculate the return for backing three or four horses in a big field if they consider those horses are the only ones with a good chance.

One of the reasons that these alternatives pop up is the chance for 'betting in running', which changes the odds dramatically. Imagine a football match where you bet heavily on a lower-league team playing against a Premier League side in the FA Cup. The minnows take a shock lead in the tenth minute. You have two choices: you can cross your fingers and hope that they hang on for a famous and statistically unlikely win; or you can go to the exchange and immediately lay the team that scored.

You will probably be offered the opportunity to take advantage of a big swing in the odds

'Build with whatever materials are at hand. The inevitable must be accepted and turned to advantage.'
NAPOLEON BONAPARTE

Defining idea...

offered and it's pretty likely that you can green out and still make a solid return. The option of hanging on, hoping for a famous big win, is a gambler's instinct. The decision to lay the leading team to guarantee a return is an intelligent gambler's instinct.

How did it go?

Q   When I take advantage of this type of arbitrage, the returns seem low.

A   *They are low to reflect the lack of risk. You don't have to win on both sides: you can just narrow your potential loss to give yourself value. In the football example, having bet £20 at 5-2 on, I can simply put £2.50 on the outsider when it drifts to 4-1. If the underdog team wins, you have a profit of £10 and a loss of £20, for a £10 overall loss. If the favourite wins, you have a profit of £8 and a loss of £2.50, for a £5.50 overall profit. You've effectively got odds of better than 2-1 on for a team that's probably now at 3-1 on or 7-2 on.*

Q   What if the market doesn't move?

A   *You can't make this arbitrage bet every time. If the market moves only slightly, the commission that the exchange takes will probably eliminate the chance for any reasonable return. The skill in this is seeing the potential for a shift in odds and striking quickly to realise it.*

40

Casino etiquette

Casinos have a mystique that can be intimidating. If you understand how they work, you'll avoid high-stakes meltdowns and bet with confidence.

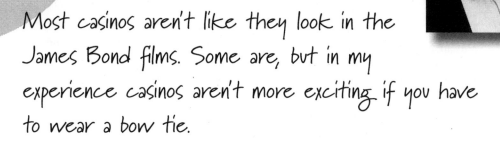

Most casinos aren't like they look in the James Bond films. Some are, but in my experience casinos aren't more exciting if you have to wear a bow tie.

The new generation of casinos that are springing up in cities all over the UK is effectively casinos for the rest of us: for people who don't think gambling is flying over to Monte Carlo once a month for a night of Punto Banco with the Marquis. Dress rules vary – you still won't get into many casinos in jeans – but a modern casino is based on the Las Vegas idea that it's more important to get as many people in as possible, and the rules are relaxed as a result.

If you're in doubt, give them a call or check on the Internet first. You'll find them spectacularly helpful in most cases, because casinos don't make money by turning away potential customers.

Here's an idea for you...

Roulette is a simple game but the etiquette relies on patience and tolerance, and that can be harder. Don't sit at the table unless you're playing. When you put your cash on the table, you will receive a pile of coloured chips. If you want a colour, ask for it; if someone else is playing that colour, tough luck. Wait until you are asked to place your bet and don't place any bets after the croupier waves an arm over the table. Don't copy players who love to sprinkle bets like confetti at the last minute. Place your bet carefully, so there's no doubt what you are betting; if you can't reach, give your chip to the croupier with instructions. When the winners are being paid out, wait for this to finish before you start placing bets again. You will know when it's time to bet, as the croupier will remove the little 'marker' from the last winning number. Relax, take your time. That wheel's not going anywhere.

When you get to a casino, it's best to know a few things about how you're expected to behave. Why? Because if you're stressed and distracted by what you should be doing, then you're not going to be able to concentrate on how to play. There's not much to know, but it's pretty important.

The first thing is that you're going to have to get inside. For that you need to become a member. It used to be that there was a mandatory cooling-off period of twenty-four hours after you join, but that's no longer the case.

On the other hand, you still have to provide ID with your name and address, and you have to be over eighteen. You can't take your kids to the casino.

Inside a modern casino, with rock videos playing, barmen juggling bottles and packed tables, there's always a surge of adrenaline. For some people, this translates into aggression, especially after a couple of drinks. This is the number-one no-no. Abusing staff or fellow players, swearing, shouting, calling people cheats or accusing anyone of cheating means that burly men will instantly eject you. If you have a complaint, complain in a civil way to the pit boss (who will be instantly recognisable). Every table is filmed constantly and if you have a case, you will be heard. However, not understanding the casino rules is no grounds for complaint. If you want to know something, just ask your dealer or croupier, and if you want to learn the game, visit a low-stakes table at a quiet time, when there's the opportunity to have it explained. Don't try and learn at 11 p.m. on a Saturday night.

When you want to play, sit down and put your money on the table. Don't hand money to the dealer directly, and don't rush in throwing money around. Be patient. You will get chips that correspond to the size of the minimum bet at that table. Don't go onto a high-stakes table if you're a low-stakes gambler: you will see the minimum stake written on a sign. Always read it before you play.

Never offer advice to other players. It's rude – and distracts you from your own game. Don't 'tut' what you consider to be bad play. For example, many players sigh when a blackjack player hits on 16 and busts. But in many cases, hitting on 16 is the best strategy, as experienced players know.

'There is need of good manners that law may be maintained.'

MACHIAVELLI

Defining idea...

When you're winning, it's exciting; whoop away, but don't get obnoxious. And when you lose, it's not because the dealer cheated you. Watch the signals at the blackjack table for players who want another card or want to stand. If you give the wrong signal, it's your fault.

Don't mess with your cards or your bets. When you place a bet, don't touch it unless you win and it is paid out. When the hand is over, give your cards but don't try to 'help' the dealer. They are trained to pick up the cards in a special way so that the security can spot cheats. Let them do their job! And never touch your cards on the blackjack table.

There are little holes in the table for your drink. Use them. Showering your fellow punters – and the table – with lager is always bad etiquette.

If that sounds all a bit intimidating, don't worry. Be polite and keep control, and you'll not only be among your dealer's favourite players, you'll win more and lose less.

Q   **I've played poker online but I feel intimidated going to play at a casino! How can I calm my nerves?**

How did it go?

A   *This is the case for a lot of online players. When you get to the casino, ask to speak to the card room manager, who will explain the rules – for example, how to put a marker on your cards so they are not accidentally folded. If you go at a quiet time, the dealer will help you for a few hands.*

Q   **How many free drinks can I have?**

A   *In US casinos, the drinks just keep coming. Tip the person who brings them one chip, or with a dollar bill. British casinos are not as generous – many will offer one free drink, and charge afterwards. This is no bad thing. A drunk gambler is not an intelligent gambler.*

Q   **Why tip dealers or croupiers? They are paid already.**

A   *They are paid minimum wage or a little bit more, so the tips are appreciated. In some cases, if you are a regular player, you may find that a blackjack dealer who you tip regularly will be slightly easier to 'read'. They have an interest in you making money. But you can't expect this, any more than you can expect a response to your tired chat-up lines.*

41

Lose the losers

When we gamble, we obsess about picking winners – but smart gamblers make a return by eliminating the losers first.

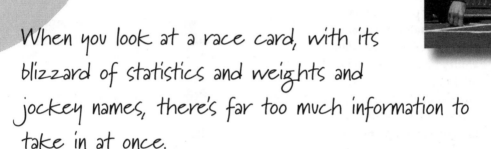

When you look at a race card, with its blizzard of statistics and weights and jockey names, there's far too much information to take in at once.

Often we let our eye be taken by simple short-cuts: this horse won on this course before; this stable is in good form; we like grey horses. Using this, we narrow it down into an arbitrary shortlist and pick from it. This is not going to make you a good return.

A more organised approach, which takes more work and planning but could see you making more reliable returns, is to make a shortlist before you look for value. Do not think about why a horse might win, but take a pessimistic view: try to find a valid statistical reason for why each horse is unlikely to win. Make your shortlist by eliminating the horses that aren't up to scratch first.

Here's the thing: the trainers and the jockeys know that not every horse they enter in a race has a chance to win. Sometimes they are looking to give it experience,

Here's an idea for you...

It's not just for horse racing: any competition where there is a precedent and form to study can yield to this type of analysis. For example, if you're betting on football teams to qualify for Europe, then their position mid-season, their form against their closest rivals or their ability to come from behind might be the historical criteria that you discover has correlated with qualification. So then you might eliminate anyone below tenth in the table, any team that has consistently failed to beat close rivals and any team that usually loses when it goes behind. That can give you an instant shortlist that's bettable, especially if it eliminates one or two of the sentimental favourites.

sometimes they are hunting for place money, sometimes it's to please the owner. The horse will try its best but we can't all be winners. And if you bet on a horse like this, you certainly won't be.

Imagine you are interviewing the horses for the job of race winner. When you are sorting job applications, you first of all throw out all the CVs that don't have the experience or expertise that you're looking for, and then you interview your shortlist. You probably wouldn't give a job to someone because one paragraph in his or her CV caught your eye. If you did, you'd expect disaster. But that random inspiration is exactly how amateurs choose their bets.

A horse comes with multiple CVs. It has its form and bloodline. Then there's the jockey and the trainer. Then you need to look at the job specification: the length of the race, the quality of the other horses, the draw and the conditions.

It's impossible to be certain when you're shortlisting, but the more work you do, the better your chances of coming up with a realistic shortlist. You will also need to take a view on which statistics are significant. So, for example, if the draw has been strongly favouring low numbers, because that part of the course is faster ground, then you can decide to eliminate all the horses drawn in high-numbered stalls. If the race has never been won by a two-year-old horse, maybe you eliminate the two-year-olds from your thinking. If a horse has been successful in slow races, but the pace is expected to be fast, take that one out of the reckoning too.

On the other hand, if the draw is favourable but not compellingly so, don't use it to eliminate a strong contender.

Do this and you'll end up with your shortlist of two or three horses. Unfortunately they might be the favourite and second favourite, in which case your analysis isn't really helping: you've assessed the same statistics, using the same criteria, as everyone else. Try to find methods that most people ignore or ignore criteria that most people give too much importance to. For example, does the distance the horse has travelled to the course correlate with its chances of success? Do horses wearing blinkers win more or less than the national average on this course? For this, you'll either need to subscribe to a firm that compiles statistics like this or else compile your own. The more work you do, the better your results will be – but it's hard work. You also need to be consistent and use the same criteria on every horse, or else you're just finding reasons to prop up your prejudices.

Maybe you'll end up with two or three horses on your list and you calculate that if you back all of them, you would still turn a decent profit whichever one won. So do that: divide your stake between your shortlist and hope that your criteria combine to be, in some way, predictive.

This isn't foolproof. It might not even be profitable at first. If you don't come up with some organised and effective method of eliminating

'Second place is just the first place loser.'
DALE EARNHARDT, US racing car driver

Defining idea…

no-hopers, it will never turn a profit. But it's a great habit to acquire: it gives you the pro's discipline not to make snap judgements and makes the research you do go a long way.

How did it go?

Q   **If a horse has just won, that surely means it's likely to win again – so should I shortlist it?**

A   *It means the horse has some quality, but look deeper and there may be better reasons for the horse not to make your shortlist. For example, what was the course and distance? You wouldn't bet on an Olympic sprinter to win the 800m as well. Is the form more than a month old and do horses that won more than a month ago win more often next time out than horses that just placed? A horse with a '1' as its last race place is a magnet for badly-prepared punters and will probably have a short price, so if you have a sensible reason to discount it, you have an edge over your fellow gamblers.*

Q   **This doesn't work. I ruled out a horse for very good reasons but it won. What went wrong?**

A   *Two things: the reasons might not be as good as you think. If no horse carrying one of the top weights from France has ever won the race, then you can potentially rule out the heavily handicapped horses or horses that have travelled from France. One or both of these factors may ultimately be important, but if neither is, you might come unstuck. There are thousands of factors that influence a result: picking just a few that will be significant isn't easy – and isn't foolproof either.*

42

Premium bonds

You don't lose your stake and you could win a million: it's not exactly exciting, but it might pay better than most of the punts you'll try this year.

The newspapers recorded the first premium bond being ceremonially bought on 1 November 1956 by Alderman Sir Cuthbert Ackroyd, which shows how old the government's scheme is, and how our taste in celebrities has changed over the years. Can't see Cuthbert Junior beating Victoria Beckham to the job these days.

Premium bonds are a relatively smart gamble. Not because they will show the rate of return that a skilled poker player or horse racing fan can show and not because there's any skill involved, but because you don't lose your stake. The winnings are tax-free and are calculated to be roughly equal to the sort of interest you would get from a deposit account. At the time of writing, the prize fund is equal to 4%

Here's an idea for you...

Why not use premium bonds as a parking spot for your bankroll? Imagine you have a bankroll of £1000. I'm assuming that you don't want all of that all at once, so you need somewhere to keep your spare cash. It's a bit fiddly buying and selling premium bonds, but there's no waiting period to cash them in (you send them a form, they send you a cheque by return of post), and there's no fee to buy or sell.

interest. You can download an application form and find out all about premium bonds at www.nsandi.com.

So why do we call premium bonds a gamble? Because not everyone gets the same return and some people don't win at all – effectively, they enjoying 0% interest, the same as stuffing the money under your mattress. There has always been a jackpot prize; for the first draw it was £1000. Again, times have changed – you'd be hard pressed to sell raffle tickets for the village fete these days with that sort of prize. There is also a few middling prizes and a lot of small prizes to keep us all interested in looking up our numbers.

Today's top monthly prizes are two £1 million jackpots – less than the lottery, but not to be sniffed at – and about one million other prizes. Calm down! There are about 27 billion bond numbers in each monthly draw (about half the adult population owns at least one bond), so even if you buy your maximum allocation you could only expect on average one or two prizes each month.

A 21,000–1 shot at winning £50 isn't an adrenaline rush. But if you like to speculate, maybe you shouldn't put everything into risky gambles such as poker, roulette and greyhounds. You need to balance your portfolio and have some safe bets, and bets don't get safer than a premium bond. Your stakes are stored by the government, so even in the advent of civil strife they're at least as safe as if they were in a bank. Every time you don't win, your bankroll stays the same. And it's quite good fun at the beginning of every month to check up and see if you have won, so you can wait for the cheque in the post.

This might not be the sort of action you're looking for. But if you are serious about making your money work harder, you have to face facts. Look at the cash you are committing to placing bets or gambling at the casino. Don't just think about individual wins, but aggregate everything you've put on over the years. Do you really think that, adding in the cost of the time and money you spent making the bets, going to the races and paying entry, or ordering over-priced cocktails at the casino, you have made a return of 4%? If so, you're doing much better than the average punter.

Premium bonds are a good example of the need to look at the big picture and examine your motivation for gambling. One of the reasons that we like the lottery is because there's a big public draw – it's an event. This might make the process more interesting for a few seconds, but don't confuse that with the return you are getting. It's hard to imagine a more boring way to gamble than buying a premium bond; there's a draw, but you don't know when and where it happens, and all you are told is whether you won anything or not – and that's by post a couple of weeks later.

So if you gamble for the thrill, there are few thrills to be found here. This is primarily a way of investing that might one day provide a big-time bonus for you. Of course, if you are a really intelligent gambler, you will even now be comparing the advantage of money placed in premium bonds against deposit accounts, ISAs and endowments. This is the class of risk we're talking

'A squalid raffle.'
HAROLD WILSON

Defining idea…

189

about. Comparing premium bonds to blackjack is like choosing between a Ford Transit and a Ferrari.

Premium bonds are a low-risk bet that don't need skill but pay small returns consistently. And they're a better bet than the other great government-approved gamble, the Lotto.

How did it go?

Q   What's the maximum investment?

A   *You can commit up to £30,000. It seems a lot, but it's a drop in the ocean compared to all the bonds out there. With that investment you'll win some small prizes most months.*

Q   Where's the skill?

A   *There isn't any. It's a passive bet, a lottery. You can't pick your numbers if you are superstitious, and there's no strategy that will help you. The only thing that distinguishes this from a deposit account is that your return is unpredictable. That might not be exciting enough for you, but if you're committing £30,000 to a more 'exciting' form of betting, remember that this is the only bet where you can't lose your stake.*

43

Lottery madness

There are many reasons to bet on the lottery, but with a 50% return on your stake, making money isn't one of them. However, if you believe that It Could Be You, here's how to maximise your potential return.

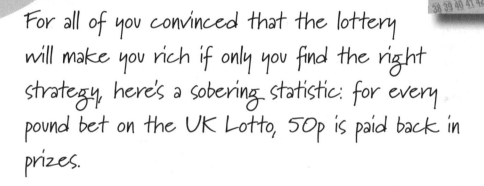

For all of you convinced that the lottery will make you rich if only you find the right strategy, here's a sobering statistic: for every pound bet on the UK Lotto, 50p is paid back in prizes.

Whatever people tell you about lottery wheels, number generators and number matrixes, you can't beat the statistics: the lottery has a house edge of 50%. It's like playing roulette with a wheel that contains a 0 in between every number.

So why do we like to play? Two reasons: the first is that every lottery has a fabulous jackpot; if all your six or seven numbers come up, you really don't care that it was statistically a bad bet.

Here's an idea for you...

Take the road less travelled. Analysis of lotteries that have permitted statisticians to look at the numbers chosen show a bias towards users picking combinations that have won in the recent past. If you don't use those combinations and you win, you have more chance of getting the whole jackpot. Similarly, when there are three consecutive numbers drawn, or two, or lots of high numbers that aren't anyone's birthday, then it is much more likely there will be no winner. So go ahead and pick your numbers based on that – just don't get your hopes up.

The second is that it's easy to play and, thanks to the way our brains work, it doesn't look as hard as it really is to pick the correct numbers. Sadly for us, in the Lotto – which we'll use as the example here because all lotteries are basically the same, although the odds are different if they're set up differently – there are 13.9 million possible combinations of six numbers picked from 1 to 49. That's big. If you play twice a week you could expect to hit the jackpot once in 133,000 years. Or here's a sobering statistic: if you're a healthy middle-aged man, you have about as much chance of winning the next lottery draw as you have of dropping dead in the next forty minutes. Quick! Get to the newsagent!

And you're getting short-changed: if you win £6 million on a fourteen-million-to-one shot, you're getting less than half the odds that any sensible gambler would ask for. It's worse if you match five numbers plus the bonus: you're getting a £100,000 payout on odds of more than two million-to-one.

On the other hand, there are not many £6 million payouts in the gambling world, and that's at the heart of the lottery's popularity. It's not exactly a crime if you pay a few pounds a week to your newsagent.

How do we reconcile playing the lottery with intelligent gambling? You could look at it as a very inefficient way of giving to charity. You should definitely look at it – as with all gambling – as fun. And if you fancy winning the jackpot, stick to rollover weeks, where you notionally get more for your money if you win. You won't win, but I don't want to crush your spirit.

Which brings me to the serious part of the discussion about lottery betting. When you're betting on horses, dogs, football teams or the weather, or when you're buying or selling shares, research is valuable. Previous trends and hidden patterns may give you clues as to what will happen in the future. There are many lottery books and websites claiming that analysing which numbers came out in the last week, or the last month, or the last year, will influence which numbers will come out this time. They point out the fact that not every number pops up an equal number of times and that some numbers don't pop up for many draws in succession. This means nothing: lottery balls aren't connected and they don't have a personality, a skill or a memory.

Here's an example from the website Gail Howards' Smart Luck (www.smartluck.com):

'Why wait for dumb luck to strike when you can use Gail Howard's Smart Luck® lotto strategies and give Fate a helping hand?' she says.

Defining idea…

'Here's something to think about: How come you never see a headline like "Psychic Wins Lottery"'?
JAY LENO, US chat show host

193

'Lottery numbers are randomly drawn. But randomly drawn numbers form patterns that are to a certain extent predictable.'

Not true.

'Six consecutive numbers (such as 1-2-3-4-5-6) have never been drawn in any state or international Lotto game. It is highly unlikely that, if it has never happened before, it will happen this week just because you put your money on it.'

This is just rubbish. Every combination is exactly equally unlikely. Lots of people probably buy the ticket with 1-2-3-4-5-6 on it because it's quick, so your jackpot would be small if those numbers came up, but that's a different problem.

'Wall Street analysts do the same thing. They chart stocks, bonds and commodities, studying past price action to determine future price trends.'

That's exactly what they do. But it's not the same thing as looking at past lottery draws, which could be the dictionary definition of a waste of time. Ms Howard offers to sell you software to help pick your numbers. Instead, why not go to the newsagent for a lucky dip? It's cheaper than the software and just as likely to win or lose.

There are many good reasons to play the lottery: it helps charities, it's fun, it doesn't cost much and you might get to be on TV. However, the desire to get rich shouldn't be one of those reasons. Concentrate your resources where your effort gives you an edge.

Q **I can bet on the Irish lottery at the bookmaker's shop. Is this good value?**

How did it go?

A *The bet that you're offered is similar to the UK Lotto, but not the same. You have a bet on exactly three numbers, for example, not on six, with a fixed rate of return. It's a separate bet to match all the numbers. It doesn't offer a huge jackpot, but it's easier to win small prizes. Yet it's still not a skill game. You can't use analysis to predict numbers.*

Q **I have been asked to join a syndicate. Is this a smart move?**

A *It's a better way to win small sums consistently. Syndicates pool the funds you pay in every week to buy lots of tickets and divvy up the prizes. So your £1 buys a share of ten or twenty tickets. On average, though, you'll still lose half your stake over time.*

44

The art of war

Gambling isn't just about reacting to what's happening; it can also be about making things happen and capitalising on that situation.

You will have realised by now that we gamble in every aspect of our lives. It's vital to separate the situations we can't change — whether a ball will fall into a particular slot in a wheel — with the situations we can. A passive gambler is not a smart gambler.

But it's sometimes hard (impossible, even) to make things happen. For our guidance in how, when and where, who better than Sun Tzu?

If your first thought was 'Who?', Sun Tzu wrote a book called *The Art of War*. He was well-qualified to do so, because he was a Chinese general about 2500 years ago. His

Here's an idea for you...

One of the most useful tactics of all is to leave your opponent with seemingly one option. 'Throw your soldiers into positions whence there is no escape, and they will prefer death to flight. If they will face death, there is nothing they may not achieve,' says Sun Tzu, who also talks at length about never surrounding an army completely. In that way they are unpredictable. When they have one dominant option, they are predictable. Suggesting a course of action obliquely, so that your opponents think they had the idea themselves, is the way to do that.

book has been an inspiration to generations of wannabe generals in the military, politics, business and gambling. Read the book – it's very short, easy to digest and it's still relevant.

We're emphasising calculations and analysis a lot here. It is vital to understand the risks that you are speculating on, to see the situation in front of you. But this is sometimes only half the story: you can change those risks based on how you act. As Sun Tzu says, 'the clever combatant imposes his will on the enemy, but does not allow the enemy's will to be imposed on him'.

This isn't always possible: few of us can alter the risk and return in a horse race or a boxing match by our actions alone. There are really only two ways to do that. The first would be to nobble the horse or the rider. It happens and, frankly, it's just a pain. When there are bribes and fixes around, we don't know about them most of the time, so we're betting based on seriously incomplete knowledge.

The other way would be to gamble such a large sum, or in such an unexpected way, that we affect the odds offered to other people. Big-time professional gamblers might be able to do this. That's not you and I.

Other games, however, you can influence. The most obvious category is card games where you are playing against other human beings whose perception of risk and reward is just as skewed as yours or mine. Our brains are wired to respond to risk in different ways depending on how that risk is presented.

But this works just as well when you're having a fiver on a game of pool, challenging your mate to a game of tennis or negotiating your bonus at work. These are gambles too and some of the gambles you make in everyday life – negotiating a house price, making salary demands or buying a new car – are the biggest bets you will ever make.

'All warfare is based on deception. Hence, when able to attack, we must seem unable; when using our forces, we must seem inactive; when we are near, we must make the enemy believe we are far away; when far away, we must make him believe we are near. Hold out baits to entice the enemy. Feign disorder, and crush him,' says Sun Tzu, and that's the trick. In this famous observation, there's more or less everything you need to remember. The basic method that most of us use to 'seem unable' is to huff and roll our eyes and exclaim 'oh no' when we look at our cards. You can only use this tactic once, and everyone does it, so it's not often successful.

Better to create an atmosphere in which your opponent will react based on what is actually happening, rather than how you are reacting.

'To fight and conquer in all your battles is not supreme excellence; supreme excellence consists in breaking the enemy's resistance without fighting.'
SUN TZU

Defining idea...

An example is the 'suck bet' in poker. You have an unbeatably strong hand with two rounds of betting to come and you suspect your opponent has strong cards too. You can go 'all in', but clever opponents will cut their losses and fold their cards. If instead you carefully and slowly make a significant but callable bet, it implies you have a strong hand but a beatable one. It's exactly what they want to see – they think they can beat you by calling it. What they don't know was you set up the situation to 'suck' more money from them.

Playing pool against someone who likes to take on long shots that they usually miss? 'Accidentally' give them long pots to try. Strap your knee before you play your tennis match if there's nothing wrong with it and don't strap it if there is. When haggling for a price, name your lowest realistic price and walk away. If you don't get called back, then your price really was far too low for them. If you do, you just earned a discount. You benefit either way.

If you want to change the situation, then gamble on your own terms. When playing against people who like to play slowly, pretend to be short of time: they still want your money, so they will speed up their play to get it – which is to your benefit. Play slowly against impatient people, conservatively against bored people and challenge irritable people. Make this your habit. As Sun Tzu tells us: 'in making tactical dispositions, the highest pitch you can attain is to conceal them'.

Q   Doesn't this conflict with the advice to always play the odds?

How did it go?

A   *A card player who waits for something to happen might wait for ever: you don't always have that time; for example, in the final stages of a poker tournament. Sometimes you need to impose your personality on others.*

Q   But you can't guarantee a win this way, can you?

A   *No. You can just help create an opportunity. Sun Tzu: 'To secure ourselves against defeat lies in our own hands, but the opportunity of defeating the enemy is provided by the enemy himself.'*

45

Using exchanges

Betting exchanges often offer much better odds than the bookies. They look confusing at first, but don't be put off.

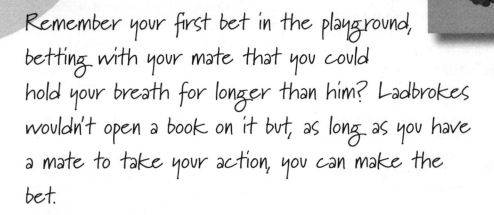

Remember your first bet in the playground, betting with your mate that you could hold your breath for longer than him? Ladbrokes wouldn't open a book on it but, as long as you have a mate to take your action, you can make the bet.

A betting exchange is a bit like a giant playground, full of people wanting to bet. As long as you can find someone who takes a different opinion to you, you can play. Betfair's role is to match people who want to make a wager. It's like a big gambling eBay.

Here's an idea for you...

To do an arbitrage comparison between a traditional bookies and Betfair, learn to quickly change decimals into odds. To take a decimal and convert it, subtract 1 from it. The odds are the number that remains, expressed as a fraction. So 4.5 is 3.5, or 7–2. To do the opposite, add 1 to the odds expressed as a fraction. So 7–4 on is 4 ÷ 7 + 1 = 11 ÷ 7, which is 1.57. Any decimal odds higher than this offer a better return than 7–4 on. Now compare five prices on bets you were thinking of making and see how many times Betfair wins.

I will concentrate on Betfair for two reasons: it's the biggest exchange, and it's exactly like all the others. When I say 'Betfair', I really mean 'all of the exchanges'.

As I write, the Green Bay Packers are preparing to play the Detroit Lions in American football. Green Bay is offered on Betfair at 1.57 (in traditional odds, that's in the region of 7–4 on) to back or 1.58 to lay. This means that if I wanted to back Green Bay to win, I would be able to click on the 'back' button and get a return of 1.57 if I won. If I thought Green Bay would lose, I could click on the 'lay' button instead.

These odds constantly change according to who is offering a bet, at what price, and for how much. The market regulates itself. It's exactly how city trading works.

The huge advantage of being able to bet 'both sides' for us is we can wager that something will not happen. Believe me, it's easier to pick a horse that won't win a race than one that will. I've been doing it for years. You can 'lay' instead of betting if you're backing a loss.

The even bigger advantage for Betfair is that if I back and win, and you were one of the customers who laid and lost, I don't win Betfair's money – I win yours, with

Betfair taking a cut of a few per cent based on how often you bet. Betfair's share gets smaller the more you bet.

Exchanges are great for one reason: the odds. Betfair claims that on average its odds are about 20% better than the ones you will get at the bookies. This varies: when I checked online, I couldn't get better than 15–8 on for Green Bay, and in most places, much less. If I was betting £100, I'd get £157 from Betfair and £153.33 from my bookmaker. The odds are better, and you can also ask for someone to take your action. For example, if I wanted to bet Green Bay at 1.6, I could enter this bet into Betfair. When someone wanted to lay Green Bay at the same price, their bet and mine would be automatically matched. If no one came along to match my bet, I'd get my stake back.

Prices are more generous because you're betting against ordinary people and they are usually far more generous than a professional bookmaker with what they offer. When you look at the Betfair screen, you see all the unmatched money to bet and lay, and at what prices that money has been made available by your fellow punters.

There are many strategies for using the exchanges, but the most important one by far is the simple piece of advice: the intelligent gambler never puts a penny on with the bookmaker until he or she has checked whether the odds are better on the exchanges first. You can do this simple price shopping by opening your Betfair window in the same browser and quickly cross-referencing.

Also, it makes being intelligent about your prices easier. If you go to a bookmaker and the price you thought was right isn't available, you either have to take a worse price or

'Look at market fluctuations as your friend rather than your enemy; profit from folly rather than participate in it.'
WARREN BUFFETT

Defining idea...

205

slink off. You might have to keep popping back to check how the prices are moving. It's really boring. On Betfair, you simply post the wager you are offering and the price you want into the giant million-bets-a-day machine that is Betfair's matching process, and check afterwards to see if some fish took the bait. On an exchange, you only need one fish.

How did it go?

Q   Do exchanges always offer better value than a traditional book-maker?

A   *Not always, but usually. The odds on Betfair are constantly fluctuating and on markets where there isn't much trading they can be very volatile. So don't simply assume that it's always the best value.*

Q   What can I bet on?

A   *Betfair has a global reach. So, in short, everything. And there are usually options in every market. For a football game there will be straight win-lose odds, a couple of handicap markets, and special bets such as the total number of goals.*

46

The vig

No, I don't know why it's called that, but a quick analysis of 'the vigorish' can separate good value from sucker bets in sports betting.

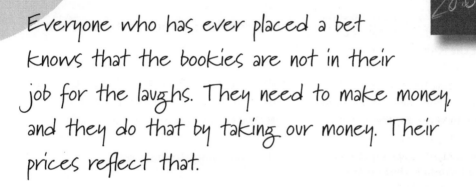

Everyone who has ever placed a bet knows that the bookies are not in their job for the laughs. They need to make money, and they do that by taking our money. Their prices reflect that.

But if you add up the prices on a race or a game, they don't add up so that 100% of the bets are paid out as wins. The margin for the bookies is called the vig or, statistically – and we're intelligent gamblers, so let's use the analytical word – the 'overround'.

Sometimes it's easy to calculate the overround or to get a feel for it from looking at the prices. This usually happens in a head-to-head, such as a handicapped rugby match. The handicaps are set up so that a draw is impossible: imagine if Bristol (handicapped at –12.5) played Leicester (+12.5). If Bristol win by 12 points, then Leicester still 'beats the spread', and Leicester's backers would win. One more point, and Bristol's punters collect.

Take the best prices on offer – choosing from a variety of bookmakers and maybe the exchanges too – for both sides in a football match or even for all the horses in a race. Price comparison websites such as oddschecker.com often carry them, as do the newspapers at the weekend. Use them to work out the overround. It's going to be very small. Sometimes, by cherry-picking the best prices, there will be a negative overround called (you guessed it) an underround. That means you can bet both sides, and guarantee a profit, although the underround is usually so tiny that you'll need to commit a lot of cash to make it worthwhile. Still, it's good for your mental arithmetic.

If the handicap is accurate – this one isn't, but as a Bristol rugby fan I reserve the right to dream – then both sides should be offered at evens, paying twice as much back if you win. In decimal odds, both teams would be at evens, or 2.0. You're not going to see that. Instead, you will see odds like:

10/11 Bristol (−12.5) vs. (+12.5) Leicester 10/11

In decimals, this means that both pay 21/11, or 1.91. Now, here's the tricky bit: that means the bookmakers are overrounding by about 5%. You calculate the overround by adding together one divided by the decimal odds for all the outcomes. In this case:

$$\text{Overround} = (1 \div 1.91) + (1 \div 1.91)$$

Which equals about 1.05, so the overround is about 5%.

The other way to calculate, using fractions, is this:

$$\text{Overround} = (1 \div (1 + \text{home odds})) + (1 \div (1 + \text{draw odds})) + (1 \div (1 + \text{away odds}))$$

Note that that's not exactly the same as the bookmaker's margin – but the lower the overround, the lower the bookmaker's margin will be. In reality, the profit that the bookmaker will make depends on punters reacting to the odds as he expected.

What use is this to us? You get better value from prices with a low overround. They are simply better overall prices, although they still might not be attractive enough for you to bet. You'll get used to spotting the attractive margins when you compare bookmakers; you don't have to grasp exactly what the figure is, just realise that 10/11 on both sides is more attractive than 5/6 on both sides.

This can also lead you to comparing the overround on different sports and even on different games. For example, certain sports or games where the bookies know that a lot of casual punters will be jumping at the chance to throw their money away will be high-margin games. Unless you are sure you have a really good edge to your analysis, it might be best to leave them alone.

Understanding the overround gives you a basic advantage. A quick calculation among the bookmakers you use will show you that, day-to-day, not all of them have the same margin – so you can learn to go first to the ones where the margin is thinnest. It is just like going to the supermarket: you expect to pay more at Waitrose. The difference is that, while you might argue the fish is tastier at Waitrose, a bet is a bet – always take the best value on offer. Also, you start to recognise the overround in simple sets of odds – for football, rugby or tennis matches for example – and you know when you're being taken for a ride, and when the prices are keen. That means you don't always have to get your pocket calculator out.

It's even possible, as an intelligent gambler, to work out the overround on a horse race – but

Defining idea…

'Torture numbers, and they'll confess to anything.'
GREGG EASTERBROOK, US writer

209

have a paper and pencil handy, as well as a calculator and maybe some aspirin. Take the odds for all the horses and add them like we did for the rugby:

Overround = 1 ÷ (1 + horse A's odds) + 1 ÷ (1 + horse B's odds) + ...

A pattern emerges: you can tell when some bookies are running at a low margin. When the vig is small, you're going to do better by taking that bookmaker's prices.

How did it go?

Q   **It's tough to work out the overround. Isn't there a simpler way?**

A   *For the bookies, no. But on Betfair, when you look at the list of decimal odds offered, there's a percentage figure at the top of the column. Usually it's very close to 100%, as it should be on an exchange, because there's no bookmaker's margin. When the underround gets significantly below 100%, it's maybe a good time to invest.*

Q   **Why should I bother?**

A   *If you want to concentrate on one bookmaker, then a bookmaker with a small vig offers you consistently better prices. Simple as that. It's at the heart of our search for value.*

47

Indian poker

You're not going to look cool when you play Indian poker, but that's exactly the point. And unlike real poker, it goes well with beer.

If some of the more technical explanations of betting make your eyes glaze over, or if grinding out a game of low-stakes Texas hold 'em just gives you a headache, or if your mates won't play poker with you because they can't be bothered to learn the rules, then we've got the game for you.

It's known as Indian poker, but some people prefer the name 'blind man's buff poker', because they're offended by the name – which it got because the card looks like the sticking-up feather in pictures of native North Americans.

Here's an idea for you...

Liar's poker is similar to Indian poker, but more complicated. Everyone has a banknote of the same denomination. Each note has eight digits in its serial number. You go round the table and each person bets, with each bet higher than the last. You bet on how many of each digit there are on every note. So the first bet might be 'three twos'. The next bet has either to be four, five or more twos, or any number of threes, fours, and so on. Eventually, if everyone challenges the bet – that is, everyone agrees there aren't that many instances of that digit – you count up the number of threes, fours or whatever the bet is. If the player wins, he wins £1 from every other player. If he loses, he pays £1 to every player.

First of all, you need friends or a family. This isn't an Internet game. You also need some beer or other alcoholic drink, preferably before you start playing, but also during it. And you need a pack of cards.

The only thing you need to explain is how to bet. The betting is the same as for any poker game – bet, fold and call – but there's only one round of betting. Each player gets one card, face down. When you have your card, you don't look at it, but you stick it to your forehead instead before the betting. In that way, everyone else can see your card except you. A tip: if your card isn't sticking, either wash your face, or lick the back of the card. For that reason don't play with strangers whose saliva you don't trust.

And that's it. The winner is the person with the highest card, with the pot split when there's a tie. Did I say it was a sophisticated game? I don't think so. But there's one aspect of Indian poker that you'll enjoy, and that's learning to read what's stuck on your head by the way people look at you and react to your bets. Also you learn about which players can be intimidated, which ones are playing without a plan, which ones give the game away and which ones are steady under pressure. You also learn how to cheat by taking the chair that's opposite some reflecting surface like a bar rail or picture, and how to cheat so well that no one spots your advantage.

If you want to bring up your kids to be just as dissolute and reckless as you, then Indian poker is a game they'll like. It's wise not to give them beer, and don't play for their pocket money or you might end up playing an unscheduled high-stakes game with the Social Services. But with that caveat, give it a go when you're on holiday and it's raining.

There are plenty of variants of Indian poker, proving that the human mind can find ways to make the most ridiculous game more complicated. There's a simplified betting version, where at the beginning, each player simply says 'in' or 'out'. The players who stay in each contribute one chip to the pot, and the high card wins.

A good variant has two rounds of silliness pre-bet. In the first round, everyone has to mock the other person's cards as abusively as is appropriate. Be careful doing this at Christmas, people get surprisingly upset. The second round of silliness requires everyone to extravagantly praise all the other cards. If you want to put in two rounds of betting as well, you can see who folds under pressure and who is susceptible to flattery.

The final variation allows you to change your card after the silliness and before the betting, and play with that one instead.

It's poker in name only, but it's more interesting than watching repeats on TV and you will learn something about yourself. Intelligent gambling doesn't always have to mean deadly serious gambling.

'There is nothing more frightful than ignorance in action.'

GOETHE

Defining idea…

213

How did it go?

Q   Isn't it all about luck?

A   *You can't control your card, but some people have a natural ability to read the expressions of other people and make the right bet or the right call. But this game isn't sophisticated enough to play for high stakes.*

Q   Is there a version where I can get very, *very* drunk?

A   *Of course. The dealer backs his card by saying how many sips of his drink he bets. (You can play this with shots instead of beer, but in 30 minutes you'll be in an ambulance, so don't.) You go round the table, and if you fold, you have to take that many sips. If you call or raise, you're still in. The player with the worst card has to take sips equal to the total from all the players left in at the showdown. This game can be adapted for the removal of clothes; but you don't need my help to work that one out.*

48

Making progress

One of the most exciting ways to play table games at a casino is by using progressive bets.

This makes your wins bigger, but also your losses: it takes a lot of control to play it well.

Progression is simple: when you win, you raise your stake. When you lose, you go back to the minimum stake and start again. You won't beat the house edge by doing this, because you can't beat mathematics. But when you win money using a progressive system, it's thrilling.

Here's how it works. You're on the Blackjack table, betting the minimum – let's say it's £5 per hand. You win: you get £10 back, a profit of £5. You have a choice: do you raise your bet or pocket the £5 for later? If you're using a progressive system, you raise your bet by a set amount.

How much you raise is up to you, but let's say that you decide to double your bet each time you win. The second hand you play for £10, the third for £20, the fourth for £40, and so on.

Here's an idea for you...

'Play with no emotion' is the advice of my local blackjack expert, Ken, who plays progressive stakes like this. He uses perfect basic strategy, and enjoys the rush of having a few monster bets every night using this system. But his warning is to always be disciplined. If you start believing you're on a 'hot streak', you'll leave your progressive bet on for too long – until you lose. And his second piece of advice: never, ever, talk yourself into progressively raising a bet when you're losing.

Imagine you win four hands on the trot. Using a fixed £5 stake, you would win £20 (four lots of £5). Using our aggressive system, you would win £75 instead, for a stake of £5. It sounds too good to be true.

Well, if you're looking for profit instead of excitement, it *is* too good to be true. The thing to remember is you can't ever beat the house odds, you can just play with the optimum strategy. It doesn't sound too extraordinary to win four hands in a row, but even if you were betting on the flip of a coin, the chances that you would guess correctly four times in a row is one in sixteen, or 6.25%. If you win three hands in a row in blackjack and lose the fourth when you're playing progressively like this, you lose the lot.

Intelligent progressive players like us don't make the mistake of chasing a hot streak until it goes cold. If you play progressive stakes over and over, you are simply playing until you lose. It will drive you crazy to see the laws of probability demonstrated like this. Instead, play a fixed progression: typically, three or four hands before you return to Planet Earth and start playing with the minimum stake again. Make this rule before you start to play and stick to it, no matter how well you are doing.

Also, if you can't bear to see those big stacks of chips disappearing at the end of your streak, use a more conservative progression. In this case, the obvious one is £5, £10, £15, £20. If you win four hands in a row, you're £50 in profit. Less than £75, but more than £20, and if you lose after three hands, you have a £15 profit as well.

One way to mix in a bit of progressive play might be to say that you will play progressive stakes only when you are well in profit for a night. Imagine you have some early success and you have doubled the size of your stack. The way that many gamblers respond to this is to simply double the size of their bet – which is perfectly fine, as long as you understand the risk of the downside. You're introducing more volatility, but it can also mean that your stack can dwindle extremely quickly. Progressive stakes means that your original bet is the same as it ever was, but the subsequent bets might be bigger. When you win, you get the thrill of being the high roller, but compared to simply raising your basic bet you are less likely to have that awful shock of reaching for three chips and discovering that you only have two in front of you.

Note that I'm not saying you will make more money this way. Progressive stakes are a way of playing for bigger money when you have that money to gamble. It's not a magic machine for making chips.

The common misconception is that with progressive stakes you win more and lose less. For statistical reasons it's not the case. Over long periods you'll still be contributing to the casino's profits with the same house edge as before. This is just the smart way to feel the fun of big stakes and the occasional big win.

'There are three classes of men; the retrograde, the stationary and the progressive.'
JOHANN KASPAR LAVATER, Swiss poet and physiognomist

Defining idea…

How did it go?

Q **Progressively raising your bet when you're losing is a winning strategy, isn't it?**

A *Not so. Think about every hand in isolation. With each hand the return will, on average, be slightly less than your stake. It doesn't matter how big the bet is, or what you won or lost before that hand. If you keep losing a little, then bet for long enough and you will lose everything.*

Q **The thrill is good, but it's depressing to lose a big bet. How can I get over this?**

A *Learn to walk away from the table without making it, then. Make a resolution that whenever you win four hands in a row, you will immediately get up and pocket your chips. You'll never know the excitement of putting on that huge stake and winning – but if you're in profit, don't complain.*

49

Online casinos

All the ways to win or lose in the comfort of your own home. You don't have to wear a bow tie – unless you want to, of course.

If you can't visit a casino, you can still play the tables. There are literally hundreds of online casinos out there, ready to take your action at any time of the day or night.

Many of them offer incentives for new players, but casino operators aren't fools. You need to gamble intelligently, because online casinos can snap up your money very quickly.

An attractive feature of online casinos for many people is the chance to literally gamble in your pyjamas. You don't have to get in your car, drive to town, fill in a form, shoulder your way to a table and then drive home again with empty pockets.

Here's an idea for you...

Many casinos offer incentives to sign up for them, usually by increasing or matching your first deposit. You can play this free deposit any way you like, but remember that you can't transfer it out to your bank after a couple of hands; usually you need to 'earn' it over time. They're not stupid, these casino owners. On the other hand, you can keep your winnings: and if you deposit £20 and get another £20 from the casino, it means you can play a lot of hands before you need to deposit more cash.

It also protects your bankroll: you don't have to pay for the 'extras'; wine and beer are cheaper at home; good food is easily available if you can find someone indulgent enough to cook it for you while you sit glued to the screen.

There are plenty of disadvantages, though. Although the graphical representations of casino games and slot machines are pretty good these days, there isn't the sheer visceral pleasure of watching the cards being dealt and the wheel spinning. Given that, statistically, you're not going to win money from the casino, the physical and social experience might be a large part of the fun – but for some people (single women, for example), not having to deal with other punters can be a real advantage.

It's also very easy to lose money extremely quickly. You can be as intelligent as you like about your strategy, but clicking on a button on your screen to bet £10 is easier than pushing ten £1 chips across a table, and that means you can lose money staggeringly quickly. In a real-life casino you will usually be asked to leave if you're too drunk to know what you're doing. In a virtual casino, there's no one to stop you, and you'll simply lose all your money and wake up the next morning wondering why the bank is calling you. You can easily spin your personal computerised roulette wheel a hundred times in an hour. Even if you bet just as sensibly as you would in a casino, where there are thirty spins an hour, you're losing money three times as fast.

Bear these problems in mind and make the online casinos work for you. Many of them offer very low-stakes or free-to-play tables where you can refine your strategy and really get to know a game, as well as long explanations of how to play. If you want to put a few hours aside to hone your basic blackjack strategy, do it online where you don't have the distractions of a real-life casino. If you're playing at a table on your own, the computer doesn't care if you take three minutes to make up your mind (or look up the correct call in a book).

Many online casinos also offer chatrooms and blogs that you can use to pick up tips from like-minded gamblers. Like any other blogs, a few are good, a few start well and run out of steam, and a lot are the outpourings of self-satisfied blowhards who think they have the secret of success.

Online casinos offer a wide range of games that you might not be able to find in your local casino too. Punto Banco? Baccarat? Let it Ride? Whatever you like, you'll find it there. Just remember: the tables might be simulations, but the money is real. Limit your hours and your bankroll, play with the same control that you would use in the real world.

> *'There is a very easy way to return from a casino with a small fortune: go there with a large one.'*
>
> JACK YELTON

Defining idea…

How did it go?

Q   Can't online casinos fix it so that I don't win?

A   *They could, and there are constant rumours about this or that casino. Be cautious at casinos that you've never heard of, but most of the big casinos use standard software that's provided by a few big suppliers. For them, a fixed casino would be death to their business if the information leaked out. And the casinos have the odds in their favour anyway – cheating to win even more would just be barmy.*

Q   I keep getting what I think is spam inviting me to sign up for a casino. Should I trust it?

A   *Be cautious of these invitations. Many are scams targeted to extract your banking details. Don't sign up to any casino, and certainly don't deposit money, unless you trust it: use www.casinochoice.co.uk to pick a casino if you don't know which one to choose.*

Q   Should I limit the hours I play? It's really addictive.

A   *Yes. Online casinos can drain your bankroll much more quickly than real ones and it's much harder to take a break. At least in a real casino you can go to the bar, go outside or go home. Try to take regular breaks and impose a maximum amount of game time every week. If you find these rules hard to stick to, you're not in control. Take a complete break for a week and think seriously whether online casinos are your thing.*

50

Variety is the spice of poker

There are many variants of poker, all with their own characteristics, where your skills might be better rewarded.

Nearly all the action today, either in poker rooms or online, is in Texas hold 'em. It has great subtlety and, often, unpredictability.

It rewards assertive play but has room for many different styles. It even makes good TV, because a camera under the table films the two 'hole' cards, so that we know what each player has. Also, it's not hard for new players to understand.

But it's not the only game in town, by any means. The basic division of poker games is in three categories. The first is draw poker, in which you have your own cards, and swap them. In cowboy films, the bad guys are usually playing five-card draw. Draw poker is fun socially but has two limitations: it uses a lot of cards, so eight players are the maximum, and four to six players are better. Also, with only two rounds of betting, you don't get the switchback reversals of fortune that you see in hold 'em.

Here's an idea for you...

You can use these other poker games to mix it up during your poker night by playing the format that's known as 'dealer's choice'. Each round of your game is played by rules that the dealer chooses – this can mean an entirely different variant or introducing wild cards. This is better when the stakes are low, because it's much easier to make a mistake when the rules keep changing.

One way to spice up your draw poker is to play 'lowball', where the worst hand wins. (You need to make rules as to whether aces are high or low, and whether you allow flushes and straights.) It certainly keeps you awake if you're used to playing for the best hand – it's a test of your mental agility to successfully play aggressively with the worst cards in your hand. If you survive that, then you could also try high-low, where the pot is split between the high hand and the low hand.

The second category is stud poker, which mixes 'up cards', which everyone can see, with cards dealt face down, which only the player can see. The standard five-card stud game deals one card down and one up, after which there is betting, followed by three further rounds of up cards. After each round, the player with the best visible hand leads the betting. This is the game played in the Steve McQueen film *The Cincinnati Kid*. There are many variations of stud poker, which all have the excitement of the hidden card or cards – but take care when you bet, as they have lots of rounds of betting.

And lastly there are the variants of 'community card' poker, where you make your hand from a combination of your own cards – dealt face down – and a set of common cards dealt face up in the middle of the table.

If hold 'em is the daddy, there's a fiendish variant that's popular online and in casinos called Omaha, which uses four hole cards per player and five community cards. You have to make a five-card hand, but this hand has to be made out of exactly two of your whole cards and three of the community cards. Don't launch into a high-stakes Omaha game if you're not used to it, because it's very difficult to read the strength of your hand – this might be one of the times when it's good to play for no-stakes until you get used to spotting what you have. The common mistake is to make a hand that uses three of your hole cards or one. As there are far more possibilities with Omaha, it also takes a much stronger hand to win the pot and it's much harder to judge when to bet and when to fold – at least until you're used to it.

If this all sounds just too easy for you and you fancy a real challenge, then play Omaha high-low, where the pot is split between the high hand and the low hand. At first, it might feel like you're always one card behind, so play for low stakes. The most common variation is pot-limit, which you will see on online sites shortened to 'PLO'. Over the many betting rounds of this variant of the game the pots can become monsters and you can lose with a hand that's almost, but not quite, the nuts. That's definitely a poker lesson, whatever the variant.

'With me, a change of trouble is as good as a vacation.'
DAVID LLOYD GEORGE

Defining idea…

How did it go?

Q **Are all hold 'em games the same?**

A *Not at all – the most important distinction is the maximum bet. No limit means you can bet anything you want at any time and it's the most exciting variant – but if you play for cash, the one in which you can really get into trouble. Pot limit means the maximum bet is the size of the pot. That can sometimes get big, but it is a more mathematical game. Limit poker has two figures ($5 and $10, for example) that are the maximum raises in the first and subsequent rounds of betting. It's much safer when you're starting out, because it's easier to calculate risks and rewards.*

Q **What is the best game?**

A *It's a different answer for everyone: different games reward different strengths. But just as it's important to have different playing styles for hold 'em, it's good practice to try different types of game from time to time.*

51

Share trading

Playing the stock market is a gamble like any other, and it's a gamble you can take part in too.

Buying and selling shares in a company has a lot in common with backing a horse or making a poker bet.

You need to do your research to find value and understand whether the reward you might get outweighs the risk of the bet. You need to have insight that isn't commonly shared. You need a clear strategy and control. And you have to pick the right moment to get the best value for your investment.

That sounds complicated, but many of us have got an investment of some sort in the stock market. If you have a pension, an endowment mortgage or an ISA, you have given your money to a large company so that it can buy shares (or bonds, currency or derivatives) with your bankroll. This is a sensible way to do things; most of the time they don't employ monkeys to do the job of a fund manager, and these guys are backed by incredibly sophisticated software that predicts how the market will move.

Here's an idea for you...

If you want to play the markets, why not try a spread bet or an exchange bet on the values of the FTSE or of currency? All the spread betting firms offer financial bets because most of their customers work in the City. Betfair has introduced a range of financial bets that combine the feel and language of a sports bet with the volatility and unpredictability of the stock market.

So that's sensible, but it's not very exciting. When you invest, the ability to choose between a Far East Small Companies Tracker fund and a North American Commercial Property Trust has huge long-term effects on your ultimate bankroll – the one that's going to buy you a yacht when you retire – but not much effect in the short term. So if you want to speculate, you might want to try the markets for yourself.

As a small investor, it's not hard to do this. Companies such as E*Trade (www.etrade.com) or even your online bank, will let you set up an account to buy and sell shares in your portfolio, and it's as simple as picking your investment and making the trade. That's the easy bit. It's harder to try and find value in a market where thousands of professionals are also looking for the same value that you're seeking.

If you're investing for the medium term – for months or years – then the biggest factor that decides whether you see a return will be the fundamentals of the company. Public companies have a legal responsibility to communicate any significant news to the market: contract wins, profit warnings or trading updates, for example. These always cause a flutter in the share price, but that flutter also translates into long-term growth or decline in the value of the company. The share price is like a bet on a horse: if lots of people want to buy the shares, the price of the shares goes up – just as if more people want to bet a horse, the odds get shorter. Strong fundamentals might not be reflected in a rise in the share price, because investors might think the stock is priced to reflect those already – just as when a horse is the favourite, it's not always worth placing a bet on it because the price might be too short.

In the shorter term, you're investing based mainly on market sentiment. You're second-guessing other investors. There are many strategies for doing this.

Range traders assume that the stock they are following trades 'in a range' – it has a high and a low price, and because the company is mature and stable, the price oscillates between the two. So the range traders buy at the low point of the historical range and sell at the high point.

Some traders follow trends: they buy stock when it starts to rise in the assumption that others will as well, forcing the price up. Others – see how this can get complicated! – like to move against a market trend in the assumption that the trend will soon come to an end. Their guide for this, of course, is the easily available historical data on the prices. For example, it's straightforward on E*Trade to call up a graph of the biggest gainers and losers in the last seven, fourteen, thirty or 365 days.

Be warned: stock markets can be incredibly volatile, reacting savagely to bad news and spreading panic as everyone runs around with their hair on fire, second-guessing everyone else. To make money effectively you need to invest substantial sums – each trade will cost about £10, as opposed to making a bet, which is free. Poker games and horse races carry risk but terms such as 'bubble' and 'crash' are special jargon for the special risks that come with trading.

'The main purpose of the stock market is to make fools of as many men as possible.'
BERNARD BARUCH, US financier

Defining idea...

How did
it go?

Q What is day trading?

A   Day trading is a form of investing that means investors 'close their posi-
     tions' – sell their shares – at the end of the day. It involves making many
     trades during that day, responding to the movement in the market. Day
     traders often invest based on news reports, 'short selling' – selling shares
     they don't have, because the price is falling so they can buy the shares
     they already sold later, at a lower price. It won't surprise you to hear that
     on nine out of ten days, traders lose money.

**Q The value of my pension fund rises very slowly. Couldn't I do
better with a higher risk strategy?**

A   Maybe for a short time. But this is an investment over decades and it
     also needs security. So pension funds will also invest in bonds and gilts,
     for example, that give a guaranteed low return over many years. You'd
     be relieved they did this if there was a stock market crash, especially if it
     wiped out your bankroll in the process.

52

Poker night

Lock the door, put your phone on silent and the beer in the bathtub, and fleece your mates. It's better than watching a Chuck Norris DVD.

It's one of those classic images of male bonding: the lads together around the table once a week, smoking cigars and knocking back a beer or two while they play poker.

This hits all the marks for classic man friendship behaviour: thinly veiled aggression, competitiveness, ritualised abuse and repetition. And it's all the better for it, say poker night veterans.

But it doesn't have to be like this. If you're a guy, you can invite girls, unless you're scared to lose to them. Girlfriends aren't there to serve snacks or to mock when they don't understand the rules. If you're a woman, insist you get invited to the table – or go and organise your own game.

Poker is a gambling game, but it's also a social game. You don't organise a poker night with your mates as a way to earn money – or if you do, they deserve better mates than you. But you want people who will play seriously; if they don't, it really

Here's an idea for you...

A really good poker night doesn't use a coffee table and a few matchsticks. Get a good set of chips, 500 or so. They're easy to find now, in shops or on eBay, and bright, heavy chips give a real Las Vegas feel to betting. Try to sit at a round table with enough space for everyone, or at least a full-height table. Your back will thank you.

cuts into the atmosphere, and you might as well go to the pub instead. It's good to play with people you know, but the same people every week can get stale – especially when you improve and know each other's game. So maybe keep a core of four or five of you, and invite others as guests – if you like them after their audition, invite them back.

Choose the night of the week carefully. If it's a one-off, choose any night where everyone can make it. If it's a regular game, you will need to plan around work, babysitters, TV shows – basically, everything that isn't poker. But if you enjoy playing, get a commitment from your fellow players and from their significant others. Don't overestimate your ability to carve out an evening regularly without a specific commitment. If you don't have a regular night, you'll end up getting together once every two years.

For scheduled nights, the day of the week matters. On Fridays or Saturdays there are clubs and bars to go to, but there's no work for most of us in the morning. On Sundays or Mondays some people prefer not to go out. This isn't a huge problem: if the day doesn't work, change it. Make sure everyone gets there early enough for a few hours of play. You don't want to exhaust everyone, but you don't want to have people popping in mid-evening when everyone is settled. It ruins the atmosphere.

I don't want to be a killjoy, but you need set rules. It's best to let players bring more money to the table when they bust, but have an expectation of how much – or how little – you're playing for so that someone doesn't bully everyone by putting huge wads of cash into every bet. If in doubt about stakes, start small; you don't want to end up betting your car keys. It's about competition, not cash. On the other hand, you play your best when you feel that the pot matters. Use your judgement.

You need everyone to know the game you're playing and any special house rules: do you play small and big blinds, or does everyone ante into the pot before you deal? You need to follow basic dealing etiquette. Don't deal the cards in twos – if the deck isn't well-shuffled, it will deal too many high starting hands. When you're the dealer, offer the cards to the right to cut before you deal, and burn one card from the deck before you deal each of the flop, the turn and the river. This isn't essential, but it's classy, and makes a fair game. Use two packs, with the person who has just dealt shuffling the pack used for the previous hand while you deal.

And you need etiquette, or things get nasty. If you win a big pot, don't grab your winnings and leave immediately. Set a break-up time and if someone has to leave before, they should say so. Don't collude with other players to bust someone: it's just rude and sucks the fun out of the game. Make jokes and take the mickey, but don't humiliate the losers and whinge if you make a bad call. And if you want to keep your friends, don't cheat.

Booze helps make the evening fun, but too much booze and it will degenerate into petty squabbles.

Good luck. And if you organise a really good game, please invite me. I'll bring beer.

Defining idea…

Leela: 'Some of my old friends from work are coming tonight for poker. Would any of you like to join?'
Bender: 'No thanks! I only play with chumps.'
Fry: 'I'm in.'
Bender: 'Me too!'

Futurama

233

How did it go?

Q   What cards do you recommend?

A   *Decks are ridiculously cheap, especially if you buy in quantity. I like the traditional Bicycle 'jumbo index' decks, and plastic-coated cards don't get ruined when someone spills a drink. Try not to use the same old cards: old decks have marks on the backs and folded corners that are easy to spot.*

Q   Who resolves the arguments?

A   *This isn't a poker room. There isn't a boss. You have to all agree about it. If there are new players, be explicit about the house rules, and you'll have far fewer arguments.*

The end ...

Or is it a new beginning?

We hope the ideas in this book will have inspired you to use your brain when you bet. Now you're thinking about your gambling more carefully you should not only be having more fun but should also have noticed an improvement in your form.

So why not let us know all about it. Tell us how you got on. What really helped you turn your 'luck' around? Maybe you've got some tips of your own you want to share (see next page if so). And if you liked this book you may find we have even more brilliant ideas that could change other areas of your life for the better.

You'll find the Infinite Ideas crew waiting for you online at www.infideas.com.

Or if you prefer to write, then send your letters to:
Beat the odds
The Infinite Ideas Company Ltd
36 St Giles, Oxford, OX1 3LD, United Kingdom

We want to know what you think, because we're all working on making our lives better too. Give us your feedback and you could win a copy of another 52 *Brilliant Ideas* book of your choice. Or maybe get a crack at writing your own.

Good luck. Be brilliant.

Offer one

CASH IN YOUR IDEAS

We hope you enjoy this book. We hope it inspires, amuses, educates and entertains you. But we don't assume that you're a novice, or that this is the first book that you've bought on the subject. You've got ideas of your own. Maybe our authors have missed an idea that you use successfully. If so, why not put it in an e-mail and send it to: yourauthormissedatrick@infideas.com, and if we like it we'll post it on our bulletin board. Better still, if your idea makes it into print we'll send you four books of your choice or the cash equivalent. You'll be fully credited so that everyone knows you've had another Brilliant Idea.

Offer two

HOW COULD YOU REFUSE?

Amazing discounts on bulk quantities of Infinite Ideas books are available to corporations, professional associations and other organisations.

For details call us on:
+44 (0)1865 514888
fax: +44 (0)1865 514777
or e-mail: info@infideas.com

Where it's at ...